Costuming from the Hip

Second Edition

by

Dawn Devine ~ Davina

and

Barry Brown

Published by Ibexa Press
www.ibexa.com

For more information about books by Dawn Devine aka Davina, please visit her website. www.davina.us

ISBN-13: 978-0615540856 (Ibexa Press)

Table of Contents

Acknowledgements

I would like to dedicate this book to Cyrena of San Diego, whose guidance and inspiration made this project both a dream and a reality. Her support of her students and the community of dance throughout Southern California is second only to her skill as a dancer and the generous heart that fuels her passionate performances.

I would like to thank all of those involved with the first edition of this book. My editor and great friend Nancy Klauschie and her husband Wolf who is much more than "just another editor." Thanks also goes out to Theresa Freese for all her help in the editing as well as her great ideas when I was first getting started. Very special thanks to Julia, San Diego's premier belly dance costume designer for her inspiration. Her style as a designer is only surpassed by her skill as a performer. She is a beautiful and talented person.

The second edition was only possible with the support of my current performance troupe, The Ottoman Traders, under the artistic direction of Antara Nepa AKA Julia Carroll. Special thanks go out to Lila Reynolds whose encouragement gave me the will to finish the expansion. Julia Carroll has been a good friend and troupe leader whose invaluable advice has improved the quality of this book. The list of Ottomans who have influenced this book is extensive, but I would like to personally thank: Connie "Kamila" Clark, Liz "Nahid" Young, Reggie "Antarrah" Stafford, Jen "Ahava" Blessing, Jillian "Lillith" Crites and Dylan Ruff. Other people I would like to thank are my good friend Sarah Bruner for her constant support and invaluable suggestions for improvements and Pat Thomas, who encouraged me to go on no matter what the obstacles. Thank you both for your friendship.

I would like to thank the three artists that made this book possible: John Sharmen, artist extraordinaire, Brian "Taras Borislav" Crites, who has far more talent than he will admit to, and Katherine Parker, who is a brilliant thinker as well as a skilled artist. I have been lucky to meet such a group of talented people!

Several of the images in the Details chapter of this book are from clip art sources. I would like to thank both Dover Publications and Stemmer House Publishers for providing the public with images useful for publication.

Last but not least, I would like to thank all of the members of SAMEDA (San Diego Middle Eastern Dance Association) and MECDA (Middle Eastern Culture and Dance Association) who have contributed tips, hints, and ideas, many without even knowing they had. I take notes constantly and owe a great debt to every dancer I have seen or spoken to in the last ten years.

However, this book would not have been possible without the constant help and support of Barry Brown. Not only did he design the layout and put the book together, but he edited all of the text and designed and managed both the Web page and the advertising. I could not have published this book without him.

From the Author

As an avid supporter of Middle Eastern dance and professional dancer and teacher, I am frequently struck by the variety of costumes available for the performer. Beautiful costumes can be as elaborate as a totally sequined and beaded cabaret outfit, or as simple as a kaftan with a scarf casually tied around the hips. Interpretations of the traditional time-honored designs reflect the spirit of the dance and the personality of the dancer.

As a professional costume designer I look at the design elements, the construction, and the details that make a total look come alive. My education includes an Associate's degree in fashion design, a Bachelor's degree in Visual Arts with emphases on textile arts, costume history, and material culture and I am currently working on my Master's thesis in Art History on the subject of costume and the Aesthetic Movement. What this means, essentially, is that I have studied costume history through looking at art. I have made costumes from almost every part of the world, from Japan to Hawaii, Peru to Russia. I have designed, draped, and drafted patterns as well as tailored costumes for theatre, living history, and all sorts of contests, but there is nothing as exciting as creating a dancing costume and seeing the performer breathe life into it. I live for the moment when the costume and the dancer fuse into one spectacular being.

Belly dance costumes are an integral part of the dancer's performance. The costume is a tool, revealing and concealing, emphasizing and accentuating, all the while tantalizing. Each dancer's personality is reflected in the choices made when creating the elements of the costume. The colors, the shapes, the motifs are all indicative of the dancer's soul. But above all, it is the dance, the motion, the life that generates the electricity which keeps this most ancient of dances so full of energy and alive in the world today.

This book started out as a collection of notes that I made while watching dancers all along the California coast and in the Midwest over the past ten years. After countless rolls of film and many sketches, I realized that this information was going to waste on my shelf. I hope that this will provide you with practical advice as well as inspiration for future design projects. *Good luck and have fun!*

Dawn Devine ~ Davina

About the Contributors

Several people contributed to the creation of this book. The talented team of writers, editors, and illustrators put in many long hours to make this book possible. The illustrations accompanying the text on this page are samples of the artists' works.

Barry Brown, editor, layout & design

A computer programmer by day, desktop publisher by night, Barry has been working with computers since 1976. Today, he works for Hewlett-Packard in Sacramento, California, and teaches at Sierra Community College. His hobbies include photography; he is trying his hand at daguerreotypy, an old form of photography made on silvered copper plates. To relieve stress, he enjoys cycling along the American River and growing plants.

John Scharmen, illustrator

John claims to be a San Diegan, though he's really originally from Riverside, California. He graduated from UCSD in 1992 with a degree in studio art. In 1993, he somehow stumbled into the occupation of video game artist/animator at Sony where he's been working ever since. He has been drawing since fourth grade, and in the *anime* style since 1985. His involvement in anime got him interested in Japanese music, language, culture, and history, roughly in that order. In 1989, he spent a year in Japan on an exchange program and he has been wanting to go back to visit ever since. He secretly would like to produce a comic book in the anime style, if he could figure out a way to do it and still eat (or figure out how not to eat).

Brian Crites, illustrator

Brian was raised in Sacramento, California, served in the United States Marine Corps, and was a peace officer for the State of California. Brian resides in Northern California with his wife and step daughter. Both Brian and his wife are members of the Ottoman Traders and the Clan of the Ax Fransisca (Renaissance guilds). Brian enjoys creating art, making his own swords and other weapons for Faire, and re-enacting many eras of history.

Katherine Parker, illustrator

Katherine grew up in various overseas countries including South Korea, Australia, and Turkey, where she was lulled to sleep by the Mevlevi Dancers (Whirling Dervishes). She received a B.A. in Studio Art & Art History at UC Davis and is continuing work toward an M.A. at the same institution. Her thesis focuses on Degas' racetrack images. Her spare time is taken up by her horse and dog and painting pictures of them and their kind.

Before You Begin

Every time a tailor or dressmaker creates a garment, they take measurements that serve as a guide for the manufacture or alteration of the sewing pattern. Before you begin, take some accurate, honest measurements of your body. Knowing your body's contours before you start will save you both time and money. Time will be saved in the fitting process and money will be saved by avoiding wasted fabric. The measurements needed will vary according to what type of costume you decide to construct. However, it is good to know the size and the proportions before selecting a design. The measurement chart is a list of measurements used during the creation of the patterns. Adapt the chart to suit your own needs but note that most of the measurements I have included will be needed for creating the designs throughout this book.

As you examine the measurement chart note the number of hip measurements. There are three here, even though most measuremeant charts include only one. Because the hip band needs to fit that part of the body tightly without constraint, detailed measurements of this area are essential. You may want to determine where you want your belt to ride on your hips and use that measurement as the top measure. Then measure 2" (5 cm) below that, and then 2" again below that. You will have three measurements that may vary widely or minutely depending on your figure type. Noting the variations in these measurements will allow you to make your belt as personalized as possible.

When taking measurements, refer to the illustrations that show where the tape measure should be positioned. Some of the measurements may seem useless or strange, but the better you know your body, the easier it will be to design for it. From time to time throughout this book I will refer to this measurement chart during the layout of the patterns. The accuracy of your measurements will directly affect the fit of the finished garment.

Sewing is a dying art. Many people do not know how to thread a needle, much less use a sewing machine. This book is not designed to teach you how to sew, but for those without sewing skills, you *can* learn. There are a large number of good books out on the market today that clearly illustrate the basics needed to sew good sturdy clothing. At the end of the book there is a bibliography that lists a few titles. Many sewing shops, fabric stores, and schools offer classes in basic sewing technique. If you have a friend who sews, you may want to work out a trade in exchange for some lessons. Don't be afraid to ask questions. Many seamstresses will share their knowledge and find it flattering that you asked. When all else fails, hire a seamstress to do the dirty work for you.

Measurement Chart

Name	Performance name
Address	Phone
	Size
	Date

Circumference Measurements

1 Head _____
2 Neck _____
3 Bust _____
4 Ribcage _____
5 Waist _____
6 Upper hip _____
7 Full hip _____
8 Lower hip _____
9 Thigh _____
10 Knee _____
11 Calf _____
12 Ankle _____
13 Bicep _____
14 Elbow _____
15 Wrist _____

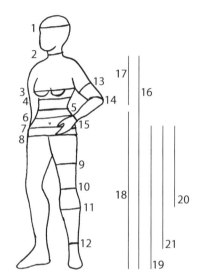

Horizontal Measurements

Across shoulders _____
Back _____
Front upper hip _____
Front full hip _____
Front lower hip _____
Back upper hip _____
Back full hip _____
Back lower hip _____
Arm length from back _____
Shoulder to elbow _____
Shoulder to wrist _____

Vertical Measurements

16	Neck to floor	Front _____		Back _____		
17	Neck to waist	Front _____		Back _____		
18	Waist to floor	Side _____				
19	Hip to floor	High _____	Mid _____	Low _____		
20	Hip to knee	High _____	Mid _____	Low _____		
21	Hip to ankle	High _____	Mid _____	Low _____		
	Inseam	_____				
	Crotch depth	_____				
	Crotch length	_____				

2 The Design Process

How does one design a costume? It is a combination of research and inspiration. It depends on mood, timing, modesty, personal style, dance style, and a whole host of other factors. Really question your needs and the goals you wish to achieve while wearing this costume. What you wear makes a statement about yourself. The audience makes judgments about the performer based on the costume they are wearing. Consequently, your ensemble should accurately reflect your mood and style. The costume you wear should be comfortable and appropriate for your particular body, style of dance, and venue. Most dancers have a wardrobe of costumes to pick and choose from depending on their audience and the style of dance they will be performing. The first question you must ask yourself is, "What style do I need?"

Cabaret bedleh

The style of the costume is the first consideration. If you want to embody the look of the Gypsy archetype, then make a list of the elements you would need to achieve that look: a full skirt, a tambourine, lots of black, and red scarves with fringe. Or suppose you want to achieve the glitz and glamour of high cabaret style, what would you include then? A sculpted bra and belt coated with jewels, sequins, and dripping with beaded fringe would be a necessity. Are you a member of a troupe? Do you dance in a particular style? Do you do folkloric style performances that require costumes from a particular region? For the purposes of this book I have broken down styles into three main categories:

Cabaret: Also known as *bedleh*, the uniform of the dance, this is the standard image of the Middle Eastern dancer. This uniform is composed of a bra, belt, skirt, and a veil. Additional accessories that match the main pieces finish off the ensemble. There are an infinite variety of design motifs and shapes that can be incorporated into the creation of these ensembles.

Fusion-tribal

Fusion: These are costumes that are composed of elements from a variety of ethnic sources from throughout the Middle East, North Africa, Eastern Europe, and India. This category includes tribal and Gypsy stylings which pull from a variety of different geographic areas. These costumes, depending on choice of materials, can look very "night club" or earthy and historic.

Folkloric: This is an umbrella term that covers a wide variety of folk costumes throughout the Middle East. This style usually covers the most skin and varies from region to region. Folkloric costumes are usually worn during specialty dances, such as the *thobe* worn during the Kalegee of the Arabian Peninsula or the *anteri* worn during Ghwazee dances of Egypt.

Elements of the Basic Costume

Folkloric-Turkish

Throughout the wide variety of garments available for the dancer, there are a few essential ingredients to creating a complete costume. Like a recipe, a costume is constructed of elements that can be mixed, matched, and substituted to create different visual flavors. By the same token, there are elements that are necessary to the finished costume; without them, the costume would be incomplete. The basic recipe looks something like this:

Basic performance costume
- One chest covering
- One hip accent
- One leg covering

For more flavor add
- One or two veils
- Scarves
- Head Piece
- Jewelry

This basic recipe allows for a tremendous amount of variation. Although you could create a costume without one of the three main elements, I am sure you would *not* want to wear it in public. The rest of the book is broken down in terms of this simple recipe. Like a chef, the designer combines basic elements and then seasons the dish with spices and herbs to concoct a fabulous meal both unique and tasty. For the costume designer, the herbs and spices are the details that are sewn onto the garments, the subtle variations between different bra strap placements, and subtle nuances in the shape of the skirt hem. While everyone can follow a recipe, the outcome can and should be different and dazzling. Designing is all about seasoning to taste. Don't be afraid to be experimental and daring.

As you go along, you might want to doodle your costume ideas. If this urge strikes you but you are convinced you cannot draw, use a copy of a nude mannequin to help you establish your ideas. Called a *croquis*, this little body guide has been used by designers since the middle of the nineteenth century to save time at the drawing table. Even if you do not intend to actually sew your own costume, this drawing will help your costume designer or seamstress see exactly what you are envisioning.

If you are skilled at drawing, you may want to develop your own croquis that matches the specific proportions of your body. Photocopy the image so that you can use it over and over again as a visual guide when doing layout and design. These little figures can also help you plan the overall lines and proportions of a garment before you begin the design process. Photocopies will save a lot of time since you do not have to figure out the correct proportions of the body each time you get an idea. So that you can have some sort of idea how this figure is used, I have included examples of how I use my croquis to graphically illustrate my design concepts. These designs appear throughout this book.

There are three things you should include on each image of a costume you create. The most important is the date; it will indicate when you made it. Second, if you are designing for people other than yourself, you will want to include both your name, as designer, and the person the costume is being created for. Use the design as a tool for choosing textiles and trim. Make notes on the design sheet about the details, what types of closures are being used, materials chosen, or sewing instructions. If you feel really creative, you can title your designs, color them in, and place them in a binder to show your friends, family, and potential buyers of your costumes. Keeping a collection of illustrations will give you a sense of how your designs evolve and progress over time.

Croquis

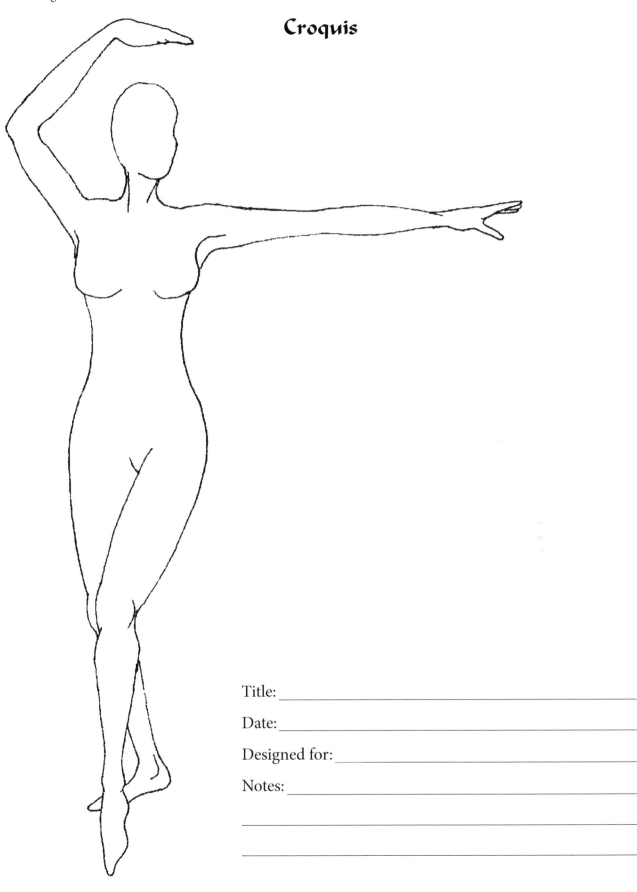

Title: _____

Date: _____

Designed for: _____

Notes: _____

_____

_____

Sources of Inspiration

As a designer, you will want to pay attention to costumes worn by other dancers. See as many performances as you can. Let them inspire your own designs. Look at what works well, but also look for elements that you may not like. Knowing what doesn't work is often as important as knowing what does. When you go to a show take a small note pad along and make notes about the costumes and how they were used in the performance. Making comments about what you did and did not like will give you a frame of reference for use when you are designing new costumes for yourself and others.

If you are a good photographer, pictures of other dancers can be a tremendous tool to stimulate your creativity. Collecting images of dancers can be a fun and rewarding hobby (but it can be rather expensive). If you see something that inspires you, write it down, draw it out, or take a picture. Later, when the creative mood strikes, you will have notes to trigger your memory and start those creative juices flowing. Viewing many costumes can give you the sense of the infinite possibilities in design, fabrics, and trims.

Collect all of the visual materials you can find on costuming and put them into a binder or scrapbook. Include a variety of garment types and styles. Don't limit yourself at first, but pick up everything you can with an image of dancewear on it. This will include your own photos and drawings, promotional materials from other dancers (flyers, brochures, and business cards), catalogues from mail order companies, articles from magazines, even photocopies of images from books. (Note: It is okay to make one copy of an image for personal educational use. If you really like the book, buy it!)

Your scrapbook will become a wonderful resource not only for your own designs, but for others as well. If you teach dance, it will be a great way to inspire your students. If you are a professional costume designer and maker, scrapbooks are a fabulous way to give your clients a sense of the range of possibilities and to generate new ideas. If you acquire great quantities of visual information, you can organize it by stylistic type, chronologically, or by source.

Anyone who has been on the dance scene knows that there are few professionally published resources available. If you see a book for sale, don't think about it; *buy*. Books go out of print quickly and you never know when you will pick up a gem. If you find yourself in the market for books, check your favorite vendor to see what titles are currently available. After thirteen years, I am nearing a whole shelf full of information. It can be a slow process, but for the designer it is worth every penny. Also, because books on Middle Eastern dance are hard to locate, the resale value is pretty high. If you get something you are not thrilled with, take it to your next workshop, festival, or sale and see if someone else is interested. If you cannot afford to purchase books, most major libraries offer inter-library loan services allowing books to be ordered from many distant sources. Also explore the options that are available in your community. College and university libraries often carry a wide assortment of books in these topic areas.

Videos are also a wonderful way to generate new costume ideas. Many artists and performers have produced high quality videos for both entertainment and educational purposes. These are an exciting resource for the costume designer as they provide views of all angles of a costume: front, side, and back. Videos are a valuable investment so take care of them.

3 **Hip Accents**

The hip belt is the oldest costume element for the Middle Eastern dancer. Small statuettes depicting dancers from the temples of Ishtar in Babylonia and Phoenicia date back to the third millennium B.C. These figures consist of women dressed in simple costumes consisting of only a round pillbox hat and a wide belt. This belt is thought by many art historians to indicate the strength and creative power of the pelvic region. The belt acts as an attention grabber, leading the viewer's gaze directly to the hips.

In India as early as 200 B.C., the key focal garment of female dress was the *mekhala*, Sanskrit for girdle. The mekhala appears throughout the history of Indian clothing as a metal belt with loops of hanging chain, pearls, beads, and precious stones. Many images of dancing temple guardians carved in stone and painted in manuscripts exist and can be viewed in art history books and museums. The drawing to the left is a copy from a sculptural group c. 740 A.D.

Traditionally, many different types of wrappings have been used by dancers to emphasize their hips. Paintings and engravings from the eighteenth and nineteenth centuries illustrate the wide variety of methods dancers have employed to draw attention to this important region. There are, however, only three major formats currently used to accentuate the hip: scarves, ethnic or metal belts, and beaded cabaret belts.

Scarves

A large rectangular scarf tied across the widest portion of the hips is the easiest way to highlight this important part of the body. Scarves can be decorated in thousands of different ways. Fringe, sequins, coins, braid, jewels, chains, and embroidery are just a selection of the vast array of decorative techniques that can be used on the surface of the scarf or along the edge.

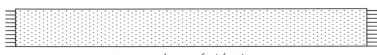

Rectangular scarf with trim

Two scarves can be used together—one in the front and one in the back—folded in half to form triangles. The larger surface area allows for a greater variety of decorations, This type of hip accentuation is depicted in the

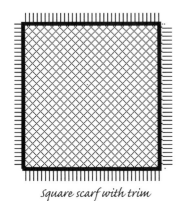

Square scarf with trim

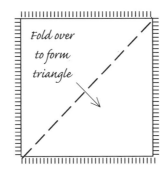

Fold over to form triangle

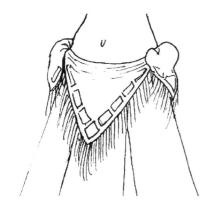

painting of the early 19th century Orientalists of France. The artistic movement of the time focused on the exotic pleasures that were available in the Near and Far East. Many images of dancers were captured with the artist's brush and may be historically accurate. Scarves are most frequently used with ethnic or folkloric costumes that bring to life the traditional dance garments from past periods.

Using scarves for hip accents allows the dancer a great deal of costume flexibility. Scarves can be layered one on top of another to form rich color combinations. In addition, scarves are very versatile costume pieces that can be used on other parts of the body as well. A large rectangular scarf, for instance, can be folded in half and knotted together a quarter of the way from the end to create a loose flowing vest-like cover. Scarves can also be used to tuck into other belts, over the head, around the neck, and, if they are not too large, around the ankle.

Decorative scarves are available in many department and import stores as well as in unusual locations like flea markets and surplus stores. Be attentive while shopping because you never know when you might find the perfect scarf. A large collection of scarves is an asset to the dancer who likes to vary the look of her outfit without a major cash outlay.

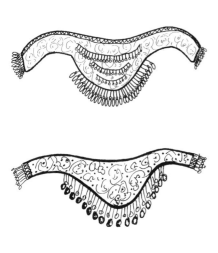

The Coin Belt

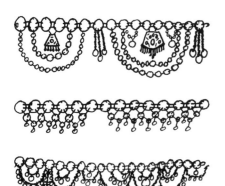

The coin belt is one that is almost entirely constructed of metal. Generally, these belts are composed of a combination of any or all of the following materials: chains, coins, medallions, gems, pearls, and mirrors. Coin belts can be worn with both ethnic and cabaret costumes, but are seen more commonly with ethnic-styled dress. You can purchase coin belts at import stores, through dealers who specialize in Middle Eastern dance wear, and at fairs. You can also make these if you have the tools needed to create metal jewelry.

Scarves are worn under metal belts to protect the skirt fabric from deterioration while in contact with the moving metal and to prevent tarnish from discoloring the fabric. The metal is also often abrasive to sheer or fragile fabrics, so consideration needs to be taken when wearing this type of belt. Sharp points and loose jump rings can catch and tear fabric, especially during veil and floor work. Before dancing, always inspect the coin belt for bent or mangled rings. Jump rings are relatively easy to replace. All you need is a pair of needle nose pliers to squeeze a new ring into place.

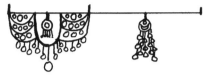

Coin belt layout in progress.

To create a belt of this type, you need a pair of pliers as well as access to a wide variety of drilled coins and chains. The greater the variety, the more you can make your belt come alive. Pieces of old tribal jewelry can be used as focal pieces in these designs. Jump rings are small round metal rings that are sturdy enough to hold two larger pieces of metal together, yet can be opened and closed with firm pressure of the pliers. There are many stores that sell chain, coins, and jewelry-making supplies either directly to the public or through mail order catalogs.

When you have chosen your materials, plot out your design on a large piece of paper. Use this pattern as a guide as you construct the belt. If you are going to be using chains, measure where the chain will lay across your body. Remember, since chain doesn't stretch, careful and precise measurements are needed. Use jump rings to clamp the chains together in permanent locations. Hooks and jewelry clasps can be attached to the ends of the belt for a reusable closure.

For a quick and easy method of making this type of belt, use two or more necklaces that you find attractive and which will hang nicely. Connect them using jump rings in sequence. The result is one long necklace—long enough to go around the hips. This is a great way to take advantage of flea market finds of old jewelry and chain belts! Bits and pieces can be recycled and re-combined to create stunning new visual effects.

Tassel Belt

Many dancers who perform in folkloric, historic, or fusion styles wear belts with long tassels. These belts are composed of a hip band that gets tied onto the body, generally in the front or at one side. The tassels are composed

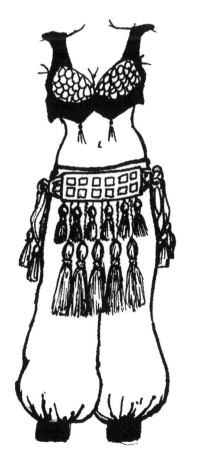

of yarn and are hung on braided yarn ropes. They are often decorated with bells, beads, shells, and other decorative items. Often the belt base is decorated with embroidery pieces, shisha, or jewelry pieces.

The first step in designing this type of belt is determining the color, quantity, and size of the tassels. The tassels are usually made by hand out of standard acrylic yarn, although if you have a supply of natural fiber yarn, that also makes very durable tassels. One method of constructing tassels is as follows:

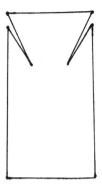

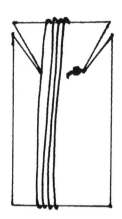

1. Determine the length of your tassel. Cut a piece of sturdy cardboard or foam board an inch (25 mm) longer than your tassel and about an inch wider than the thickness of the tassel skirt. Cut two slits into the board as shown in the diagram. These slits will be used to secure the initial and final threads.

2. Tie a knot in the end of the thread, anchor it through one of the slits, and begin wrapping. Wrap until you have achieved the desired thickness. Tie a knot in the end and secure it through the other slit.

3. Pass a thread about six inches (15 cm) long under the wrapped threads; using a large needle will make this easier. Tie a sturdy knot at the top. You will tie your hanging cord to this short thread. Cut the loops at the opposite end of the tassel.

4. Create the collar by using a thread twelve to twenty inches (30–15 cm) long, depending on the thickness of the collar desired. At the end, knot the yarn and tuck the end under the collar.

5. Trim the skirt so the tassel is nice and even. A rotary cutter works wonderfully for this. You may want to string beads onto the hanging cord at this point.

After you have constructed a number of tassels, you will want to stitch them to a base. To make the base, start with a length of heavyweight fabric whose length is four inches (10 cm) less than your hip measurement. Fold in half lengthwise, then fold each of the edges inward about an inch. Stitch this together. Attach two softer pieces of fabric at both ends to form ties. The tassels can be stitched onto the back of the belt or directly into the seam as it is sewn shut. Decorate the band as you desire. For more stiffness, add interfacing to the band before sewing shut.

Tassels can also be hung from a thick braid made from the same yarn as the tassels. Each strand of the braid is composed of several strands of yarn, as many as ten, but this is really a matter of taste. The bundles get braided together to form the belt base. The tassels are tied onto the braided belt. Decorations can be added and the braid can be made with as many bundles as you like—the more bundles, the wider the belt.

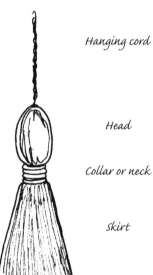

Hanging cord

Head

Collar or neck

Skirt

Cabaret Belt

This type of belt is worn by dancers performing in restaurants and clubs. Also referred to as the hip girdle, the cabaret belt is often elaborately decorated with sequins, beads, mirrors, gems, fringe, coins, and braid. They typically have a matching bra that echoes the belt in materials and design. Belts of this type are thick, heavy, and very snug-fitting. Because they are stitched together out of fabric, many different shapes can be achieved on the lower and upper edges. This belt type allows for the greatest creativity of the designer.

There is no one set method for constructing this type of garment. Every designer has her own secrets for stiffening the belt, securing the decorations, and techniques for achieve the perfect fit. Ask other dancers how they achieve their fabulous costumes and they may share with you their secrets if you share a few of your own!

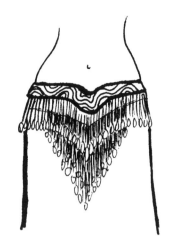

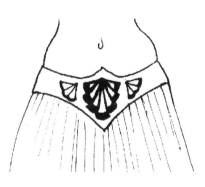

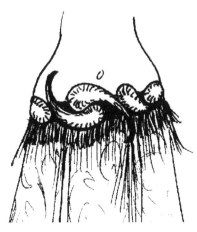

Begin with a clear idea for the design of your belt. Consider where it will close, what type of trim you will use, and where the stress points will need reinforcement. The decorations can be an important factor in deciding how thick the stabilizing layers need to be. Coins and chains are much heavier than fabric, fringe, or ribbons and may pull or stretch even heavyweight cloth.

Designing Your Cabaret Belt

Being less constrained by history or tradition, with a cabaret belt you can let your imagination and creativity go wild. When you begin designing, consider how you are planning to decorate the top. Because belly dance costumes frequently have matching bras and belts, you should design the basic silhouette of both at the same time. By designing them together you assure that the two costume pieces will match by incorporating the same design elements and materials.

Begin by making some decisions about the shape of the belt. These belts can have virtually any shape you like on both the top and bottom edges. I have included some sample designs with the features commonly used by dancers today.

Front closure with central motif. In this belt style, the closure is at the front of the belt, usually centered, but can be asymmetrical as well. The centered design offers the viewer a visual balance, breaking the body into two equal halves. Asymmetrical designs will draw attention to one side and can be modified easily if the dancer's weight fluctuates. The central motif is often a simple geometric shape but it can also be a stylized abstract form or a floral image. See the section on motifs for ideas.

Side closure with balanced front and back. In this style, the front and back have a very similar shape and design, often with the back being larger to cover the wider span of the buttocks. This is a very common style that is easy to create and is often the choice of first-time belt makers.

Stylized or irregular upper and lower edge. In this style, the designer takes total freedom when chosing the line. The closure can be placed wherever the pattern allows, though side or front closures are easiest for the dancer to put on. Because the belt is made from various types of fabric, they can be cut into any irregular form or shape imaginable. Similar forms along the edge of the bra completely unify the look. Chose any form or motif to repeat along the entire belt.

There are a multitude of design opportunities available to the creative designer. These are just a few suggestions, and should by no means be considered a full or complete list of design variation. Do what is right for you or the dancer you are designing for. Consider the body type and whether you are trying to conceal any imperfections or emphasize advantages. Also think about how low you really want to go. There are many different heights that are acceptable in the realm of the dance world. From the *ultra high* (an inch below the belly button) to the *ultra low* or anywhere in between, the belt should suit the modesty level and body consciousness of the performer.

The decorations may also play some part in the design of the belt. If you are planning on placing fringe on the belt, you may want to keep the lower edge rather simple because the fringe will cover the design. If you have some appliqués to incorporate into the design, you may want to shape a central motif to fit the piece exactly, or you might cover your entire belt with the appliqués, in which case the top shaping line can be altered to exactly fit those shapes. Lining the appliqués and stitching in a thin piece of wire for stiffening will keep those shapes in place. There is more information about choosing outer decorations in the design elements and materials portion of this book.

Belt Pattern Design and Layout

Now that you have an idea of what you want the belt to look like, you can design the pattern. There are two basic methods for belt design: adapting a pattern or with duct tape. You will have to experiment to find out which approach works best for you. Try on as many different belts as you can find and take note of the styles that most appeal to you and flatter your figure.

Method One: Duct Tape

This method I call the tape-it-up-and-cut-it-off method. For this technique you will need a roll of masking or duct tape, an old tee shirt that extends below the hips, a pair of shears for cutting through the tape, a pencil, and a friend. The friend is an important element of this design method. You will need him or her to place the tape and the cut the pattern.

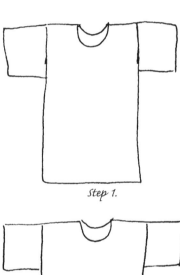

Step 1.

1. Put on a close fitting leotard or bathing suit. Put the old tee-shirt over that and let it hang loose. Do not wear pants! Tights are okay, but make sure they do not add too much bulk in the hip area.

2. Wrap yourself in the tape starting at an inch above the desired top line down to an inch below the bottom line. Make sure the tape is pulled as tightly as possible next to the skin, as a close fit is what you are after.

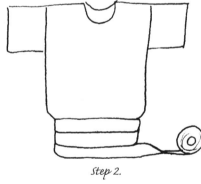

Step 2.

3. Once you are completely wrapped, have your friend mark the center front, center back, and both side points. Draw the shape of the top line and the bottom lines and the closure on the tape. Label all of the markings so that they can be identified when they are off your body.

4. Starting at the hem of the T-shirt, cut up through the tape. Cut at the point marked for the closure. Continue cutting until you are through the tape. Cut around the body just above the tape line to free the taped portion from the body. **Be careful!** Don't cut anything you don't want to cut. Be careful of cutting the leotard and the body beneath it.

5. Lay out the taped pattern and go over the markings to make them smooth. Cut out the drawn pattern and transfer it to paper. If the curve is very sharp, you may have to cut slits into the pattern. Mark these slits when you are transferring the pattern to paper as large V's running from the top line to the bottom. These will become darts during the creation of the garment.

Creating the pattern can be very frustrating. Take a deep breath if you get nervous and tense. The creation of a costume is an act of love and like most acts of love, there is a bit of emotional stress. Remember that Rome wasn't built in a day, and neither were you. You are going to have to spend time creating your belt as well.

Step 3.

Method Two: Adapt a Pattern

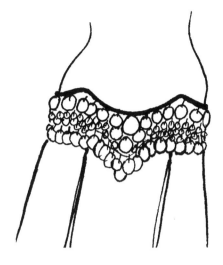

Another option is to use an existing belt pattern. You can use a belt from another dancer who has a similar shape and measurements to your own and trace the outline to use as a pattern. You can buy patterns from companies that sell patterns specifically for Middle Eastern dancing costumes. You can also turn to the appendix on belt patterns for a few basic sample patterns that you can adapt and redesign to fit your needs.

If you use an existing pattern, these features will help achieve the perfect fit:

1. The belt pattern should have a slight curve to it. Your body curves, so the belt should curve as well. The exception to this is if your hip measurements are very close or if the belt is very narrow (between one and two inches).

2. The pattern should have enough overlap to comfortably secure the belt. If it is a wider belt, you will need several hooks to fasten it.

3. Make sure that the belt is wide enough to cover everything you need to cover. If you widen it, you may need to adjust the curvature and measurements.

No matter how you acquire your belt pattern, remember to test it out using a sample piece of fabric *before* you cut into your final fabric. This may seem like a lot of work. However, it will save you money by allowing you to correct any serious flaws before you use your expensive fabric. It is a good idea to make an entire sample belt from start to finish to perfect your skills and see where problems arise. The sample belt can then be used for practice or to wear to classes. Use the same type of interfacing and a similar texture fabric that you plan to use on your final belt so that you can get an accurate idea of the belt making process.

If you have some experience using the draping technique, you can utilize it to create a pattern. There are books on the market that will step the novice through this process, or you could take a class on this technique at your local community college. Check the bibliography for sources.

Fitting the Belt

The easiest method to use to achieve a perfect fit requires two sets of hands. Make the back and the front of the belt as two separate units. One person holds the back of the belt in place while the helper positions the front to the perfect angle and position. The two pieces are then pinned in place. At this point you should try moving around while wearing the belt. How will it act when you sink down in a knee bend? Does the belt pucker? Does a gap appear at the top or does it sag? It shouldn't move. The goal is to make it fit like a second skin.

Once you have fitted the belt, machine stitch one side together leaving an overlap on the other side for the closure. When you lay the belt out, there may be an angle where the front and back meet. Only after you have achieved the perfect fit can you move onto the fun part, covering your cabaret belt.

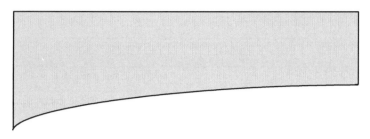

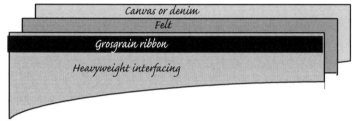

Canvas or denim
Felt
Grosgrain ribbon
Heavyweight interfacing

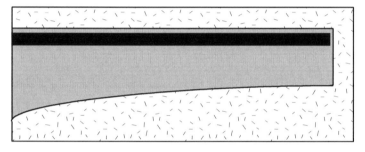

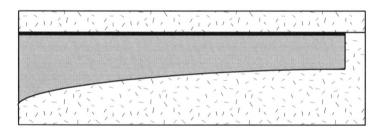

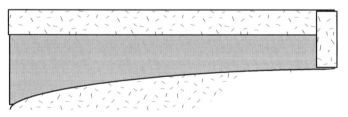

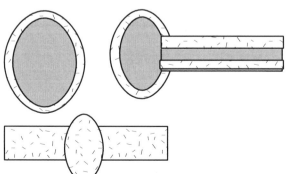

Covering Your Cabaret Belt

Once you have chosen your design and have the pattern for your belt, you can cut it out and stitch it together. Use these steps as a guide. The illustrations depict a very simple center/front closing style with a central motif over the closure. A pattern for the illustrated belt is located in the belt pattern appendix at the end of the book.

1. Pad the belt and add the interlining. Standard interfacing alone is usually not strong enough to support the decorations and prevent stretching of the belt. A typical belt might have a layer of interfacing to stabilize the outer fabric, a layer of felt to give support beneath the interfacing, and a layer of hair canvas to prevent stretch. Cut these layers out of the pattern with no seam allowance. In addition, cut a strip of grosgrain ribbon to provide an extra anti-stretch support at the top edge of the belt. Stitch these layers together by machine or with small, even hand stitches.

2. Cover the belt with the fashion fabric. Cut the outer fabric two inches (5 cm) wider than the belt all the way around. Fold the edges over the belt and hand stitch the main fabric down. Hand stitching will give a smooth finish on the outside of the belt. However, if you are planning on covering the entire belt with decoration, you can sew the top fabric on by machine because the stiches won't show.

3. Add the central motif. Attach the central motif to the end of the belt. This motif should be constructed in the same manner as the rest of the belt. In addition, you may want to add an extra stiffener like plastic canvas or an edging of wire for even more support. Fit the belt to your body and attach hooks and eyes for the closure.

Once you have made the belt, you can begin decorating it. Use your creativity to come up with designs and materials. Refer to the drawings you have made as a guide for the applying the decoration. If you need a few pointers, check the chapter on details for more ideas and information on belt decoration.

4 Chest Coverings

The chest must be covered if Middle Eastern dance is to remain a family activity. As soon as the whole bust is exposed, you have ventured into new realms of exotic dance. Even so, dancers take great pride in displaying their bodies to the greatest advantage. Cleavage is acceptable, and for many devotees of the dance, required. Accentuating, while at the same time covering, the bust is the primary goal of most dance costumes.

The design of the chest covering should match or harmonize with the construction of the hip accent. The same or similar materials should be used to create a visually unified costume. If the bra or vest does not match the belt, it gives the viewer an uneasy sense of incompletion. There are designs that can push this rule to extreme limits. For instance, when a metal belt is worn on the bottom, the top may not exactly match. In cases like this, the goal is to create a visual harmony between the upper and lower costume elements.

There are several different formats for chest coverings, depending upon what image the dancer is trying to create and how revealing she desires her costume to be. The dancer needs to consider the advantages and limitations of each style before choosing one. Although there is a tremendous variety in the styles of tops available to the dancer, there are only four main types: the loose blouse, the fitted choli, the vest, and the bra. Another possibility is to combine differing tops and bottoms into a unified whole. For those styles, turn to the chapter of this book on combinations.

The Loose Blouse

Blouses are loose-flowing shirts that can be styled in a variety of different ways. The contemporary blouse is just a highly evolved style that began in the Middle Ages as the chemise. During that period, shirts shaped in a simple "T" format were worn under finer outer garments as a means of saving wear and tear on the garment as well as avoiding damage to the fabric from excess perspiration and body oils. The blouse could be washed more frequently than garments made of more opulent fabrics such as velvets and brocades.

Blouses that end at the midriff with long flowing sleeves are often worn with Gypsy-inspired dance costumes. This type of blouse is an inexpensive covering that can be made of a variety of materials ranging from cottons to silks in lightweight or middleweight weaves. Knits can be used, too, if they are not bulky and drape well across the body.

The standard blouse is made from four pieces: front, back, and two sleeves. Elastic holds the garment close to the body at the midriff hem, the neckline, and at the wrists. Slits can be placed in the sleeves and the height of the neckline can be varied to alter this simple design. Color, pattern, and choice of materials are what really makes this style distinctive and special.

This style is nice for those women who wish to camouflage their arms and upper back region. The blouse is also good for the beginner who wants something which is comfortable and fun to wear to dance classes, yet is easy to clean. It can be layered with other costume pieces like an *anteri* or a vest to change the look and extend the lives of those tight-fitting garments. Depending upon the materials chosen for this style, a blouse can be constructed to last for years, even when washed frequently.

Making the Blouse Pattern

1. The first step is to draw the sleeve pattern. The first line will be part of the neckline. This should be between eight and twelve inches (20–30 cm), depending on how full you want your garment.

2. Now measure from the side of your neck to your wrist. Draw a straight line, perpendicular to the first, and make it the length of this measurement plus three to five inches (8–12 cm). The more length you add, the more your sleeve will droop past your wrist.

3. Measure from the side of your neck to the fullest part of your biceps. Mark this spot on the long center line. Now measure your biceps and add two to six inches (5–15 cm). This will determine the fullness of your sleeve. Draw this length on your pattern at your biceps mark.

4. Now connect with a straight line the end of the biceps mark to the end of the neck mark. This angled line becomes your arm opening.

5. The front and back can be made from the same pattern piece. Decide how full you want the fabric to be gathered over your bust. Most tops have a front that is between ten and twenty inches (25–50 cm), depending on fullness. Mark the center point on this line.

6. Lay your sleeve pattern on top of the front/back pattern to transfer the angled arm seam line.

7. Measure down from the edge of your arm seam to where you would like the blouse to end. This should be at least four inches (10 cm), and depending on the fullness of your bust line, could be as many as ten to twelve inches (25–30 cm).

8. Add seam allowance to the sides and arm hole seams. Add two inches (5 cm) to the top and bottom edges for the casing.

9. Stitch the sleeves onto the fronts and backs. Stitch the sides seams together. Fold over the casing and press flat. Stitch the casing up leaving an opening to run the elastic through. If you are going to use ties, you will want to add a button hole or grommet to allow the tie to hang on the outside of the blouse. Trim as desired.

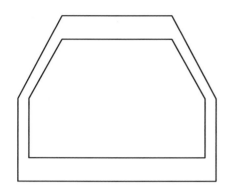

Blouse body

Blouse sleeve

Make sure to test this pattern out on inexpensive fabric to make sure it fits. If it is too tight, add width around the body; if the sleeves are too long, shorten them. If the shirt is too short or too long, make the changes now before cutting it out of expensive materials. Many performers like to vary this design with different sleeve lengths, ruffles, and decoration on the neckline, as well with different textiles. Use your creativity to come up with a style that you like to move and be seen in. Check your local fabric store to see if there is a similar-styled pattern currently in one of their pattern books; it frequently appears in their summer collections.

The Fitted Choli

Popular among historical re-enactors and tribal style dancers, the choli is a versatile garment that can be made out of different fabrics to achieve different looks. This garment is Indian in origin and the word choli means blouse. Cholis are worn under the *sari*, and historically, Nauch dancers wore the choli with a full skirt. There are numerous variations of the choli throughout India and amongst dancers as well.

The choli has several distinctive features. First, it is frequently backless, with ties at the neck and at the hem that hold the garment together. Cholis come with short or long sleeves, but they are usually fitted and are cut from rectangles of fabric. A gusset is necessary to allow freedom of movement. Historically, women have not used patterns to create their garments, but instead used older garments as models and draped the garment to fit. Experiment with different techniques for constructing and designing the choli.

The Choli

This style is very simple and is not very fitted. In fact, it is little more than a variation on a halter top. The key to this choli is measuring your bust fullness—a measurement that most garments never require. What you will do is measure from one side of the breast to the other over the fullest point. This measurement will become the basis of this choli.

1. Take your measurements. You will need rib cage measurement, your biceps measurement, your bust fullness, and shoulder-to-ribcage going over the fullest part of the bust.

2. Your ribcage band should be four inches (10 cm) wide by your rib cage length. If you are going to close it with a hook and eye, add two inches (5 cm). If you are going to close it with ties, add at least fifteen inches (40 cm). You may want to add more and then cut them to the proper length after the garment is done. Fold under 1/2" (15 mm) along both long edges and press. Fold in half lengthwise and press again.

3. Create the front by using your body measurements. Use your neck-to-ribcage measurement to determine the length of the piece, adding 1/2 to 1 inch (15–25 mm) for ease. Use your bust fullness to create the bottom width. Add an inch or two (25–50 mm) to this measurement for ease. At the side, draw a straight line perpendicular to the bottom three to six inches (8–15 cm) up, depending on the fullness of the bust. At the top, determine your width; it could be as little as 3" or as wide as your shoulder line. Draw this line in. Draw an angled line from the front to the shoulder and from the side to the shoulder. The pattern should be shaped like the example shown.

4. The back can be any width that you are comfortable with. If you have a beautiful back, make the back strips 3" or less. If you want to cover more of your back, these can be made 5" or 6" (13–15 cm) wide at the bottom to make them slightly tapered rectangles. Lay this pattern piece over the top, lining up the bottom edge. Mark the side seam height.

Traditional choli back style.

5. The sleeve is a rectangle. Measure the fullest part of your arm, usually your biceps. You can make this sleeve any length you like.

6. The gusset is usually a 5" (13 cm) square, although for a larger garment you may want to go as large as 6 1/2" (17 cm). For a smaller garment you may want to make the gusset smaller.

7. Make sure to add seam allowance to all pieces. Use the amount that you are used to. Some people prefer 5/8", some people prefer 1/5".

8. Construct the choli. First, pin the side front and side back together and stitch. Next, stitch the shoulder seams together. Line up the center of the sleeve with the shoulder seam. Stitch the gusset to the top of the sleeve. Turn the sleeve inside out, stitch up to the start of the gusset, and then turn and stitch gusset. Turn the sleeve right side out. Pin the sleeve into arm hole, lining up the bottom of the gusset with the side seam. Finish the neckline and back by making a rolled hem or covering with bias tape. Attach the ribcage band by slipping it onto the front pieces, lining up the two front edges. Stitch the band closed. Add ties to the top across the back about 2–3 inches (5–7 cm) lower than the shoulder line.

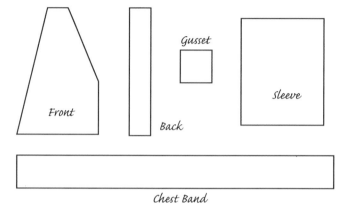

Chest Band

Like all of the pattern layouts, make sure that you try this out in an inexpensive fabric and then adjust the fit before using better quality materials. If the neckline is gapping away from the body, adjust the shoulder line, bringing the seam lower. If you want a more fitted style in front, you can make the choli as instructed but when you have the sides, the sleeves, and back all stitched together, you can put the choli on inside out. At this point, you can make a fold under the breast. Stitch this fold down and it will become a dart, thus making the style even more closely fitted.

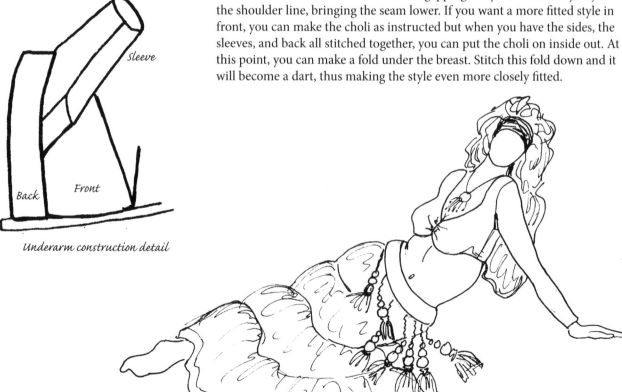

Underarm construction detail

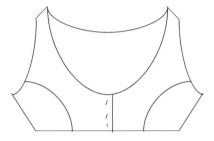

The pieces of the vest. Right: basic design for front and back, left and right. Left: the front pieces have cutouts for the neck and arms.

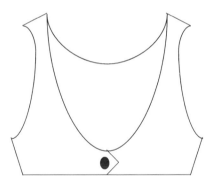

Tailored vest.

The choli is a very personal garment based on your own measurements. The choli can also be made out of knit fabric or cut from a long-sleeved leotard pattern that you can purchase in any fabric store. Many Middle Eastern dance suppliers also carry patterns for the choli. You can buy them pre-made in some Indian import stores and from dancewear vendors.

Hint: Understanding Gussets

The gusset may seem like a foreign element in clothing. Western clothing relies on the principle of tailoring to get the correct fit. A jacket, blouse, or shirt is cut and stitched to conform closely to the curve of the body. An example of this is the rounded arm hole. Sleeves are then set into this curve with additional fabric added to the top, back, and underarm areas so that you can move your body without straining the fabric. Traditional Middle Eastern clothing is based on the "T" shape. Here the integrity of the fabric is more important than a tight fit. The arms and bodies of the garments are cut with straight lines. As you might imagine, the highest you can raise your arms without strain is into a "T" position. The moment you have to raise your hands above your head, a strain is put along the side seam and across the chest. To avoid this strain, extra triangular- or diamond-shaped pieces are added to the underarm seam where it meets the body. This gusset allows for greater freedom of movement while still maintaining the smooth line of the fabric. The other alternative is to leave the underarm area open. This is good for ventilation but the view can be the pits.

The Vest

Periodically, vests are singled out by fashion designers as the focus for design experimentation. For the Middle Eastern dancer, vests are a versatile costume element that can be incorporated into a variety of looks. Because it is relatively small, the vest uses less fabric and is thus less expensive to create. Very expensive textiles can be used in a cost efficient manner, or scraps can be pieced together to form new and innovative designs.

There are two basic styles of vest: the tailored and the untailored. Tailored vests have a princess seam or dart that allows room for the bust. The untailored vest doesn't have this feature. Instead, the untailored variety cuts below the bust and is worn with a blouse or bra or, if cut higher, presses the bust straight into the body, accenting or creating cleavage.

If you plan on making a fitted, tailored vest, I recommend buying a standard vest pattern from one of the major pattern manufacturers and adjusting it to the desired shape. As long as the darts or princess lines are on the pattern, all other elements can be adjusted with ease. Lowering the neckline and raising the waist are simple.

Don't be afraid to experiment with the cut and fit of existing patterns. They are there as a guide for your creativity, not as rules that you must follow. Redraw lines as you wish. Just remember, the most crucial seam is the princess line that passes directly over the bust. Test the changes you make in a sample fabric to prevent losing money on mistakes in your final fabric.

Untailored vest.

The Bra

The beaded and sequined bra has become an expected part of the cabaret costume. It serves as a uniform that identifies the Middle Eastern dancer. The bra is, however, a Western development. Dancers in the Middle East wear bras now, but they were not invented there. The bra style is the most revealing and thus one of the more erotic styles of Middle Eastern dance apparel. A dancer must have a good sense of body confidence to wear a revealing bra. If you do not feel that you are ready to show it all, there are additions you can add to the bra such as arm drapes, sleeves, and epaulettes. Vests can be worn over the bra or a combination which will cover body parts that the dancer may feel are less presentable. Only dancers who are comfortable in such a revealing costume will look comfortable dancing. Know thyself and what you do and don't want to reveal.

The cabaret bra comes in a wide variety of styles and shapes that work to emphasize the bust area by either highlighting the dancer's endowments or by creating the illusion that there is more there than there actually is. Cleavage is the key; how much to show is determined by the style and cut of the bra. This is one time when stuffing can be taken out of the sock drawer and raised to an art form. Every dancer evolves her own tricks for achieving the shape she desires, either by minimizing or maximizing, or through special effects. The bra is the one of the most difficult costume elements to fit due to the different curves and pliable volumes of this part of the female anatomy.

Bra Buying Tips

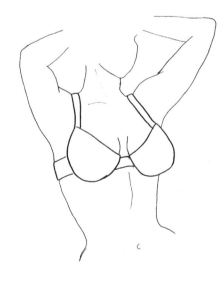

The cabaret bra is actually an adaptation of an existing hard-cupped bra you can purchase through Middle Eastern dance costume suppliers or from a department or specialty store. When you are ready to purchase your first bra, plan on spending some time looking around for which types and styles are offered in your area. Push-up and cleavage-enhancing bras periodically experience fashion revivals. When they do, stock up. Many stores only carry hard-cupped bras during the holiday and prom seasons. Strapless bras often come with hard cups and are available in the summer. Often, the add-a-size bras come with a firm layer of fiberfill that gives a larger, fuller look. These bras make excellent bases for cabaret styles for the performer who wants a little more coverage than the strapless varieties provide. In either case, here are some features to look for when shopping for the bra base:

Fabric: Look for a densely woven fabric or a tight knit that resists giving when you pull against the fabric. Remember that this bra has to support not only you, but the decorations as well. The firmer the fabric, the more decorations can be added to the bra.

Underwire: Even if you do not normally need an underwire, in the cabaret style bra it is essential. The underwire contours and supports the base of the cup. It helps to keep the cups where they belong so that you will not slip out. In addition, the underwire provides support for heavy layers of trim that otherwise would distort the shape of the cup and assists the dancer during movements which would otherwise look less controlled. It is better to buy a slightly wider wire than you need and add some padding than have bruises from wires that are too narrow.

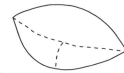

Step 1.

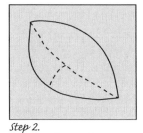

Step 2.

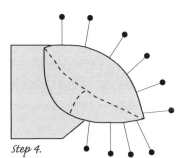

Step 3.

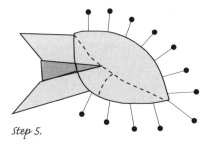

Step 4.

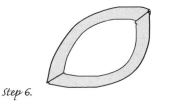

Step 5.

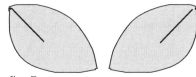

Step 6.

Step 7.

Shaping: Make sure that the bra covers everything that needs to be covered. Some strapless bras are quite tiny when they are actually worn. Even though you will cut the straps off the bra, try it on at the store and test the coverage. Make sure that it doesn't dip below your modesty level before you invest time and money into the decorations.

Finally, when you do find a bra style that you like, fits well, is flattering, and is strong enough to use as a base for beading, buy several and stock up. Bra styles come and go with the fashion trends. Having a stockpile will guarantee that you will have a perfect bra for your next costume.

Covering the Cabaret Bra: Step by Step

1. Begin by removing the straps from a standard bra, leaving only the cups.

2. Cut two pieces of the covering fabric 2 to 3 inches (5–8 cm) larger than the cups.

3. Beginning at one corner, gently fold fabric over the top of the cup, pinning as you go around.

4. Continue pinning the fabric. Be sure **not** to pull too tightly on the fabric. The cup can lose shape and definition, causing it to buckle if the fabric is pulled too tightly. You may find it helps to push the cup out and hold it in the proper shape. Be firm but gentle.

5. As you return to the starting point, you will find you have an excess of fabric. Create a dart by gently folding the fabric under.

6. Stitch along the inside of the cup, tacking down the covering fabric securely. Stitch the dart down on the outside of the cup as well. Cut away any unnecessary fabric, leaving an even hem around the inside of the cup.

7. Repeat steps 3 to 6 with the other cup. Make sure that you begin pinning on the opposite corner. You will want the darts to be on the outside edge of the cups.

Straps

Once you have covered your cups you will reattach them to the straps, putting the whole bra together. You may want to fully decorate your cups with beads and trim for ease of handling before you put the straps on. Some performers prefer, however, to put the straps on to assure the fit before they decorate. This is a personal choice.

There are many options for putting straps onto the dance bra. There was a time when the halter version was the industry standard. However, the halter can cause neck strain, especially in dancers who are well endowed. To prevent damage to the neck, there are several alternative methods for attaching straps. Experiment with grosgrain ribbon, pinning the straps into place with safety pins and trying the bra on. Unfortunately, there is no magic to putting on straps. Rather, it is a matter of trial and error. Experiment until you find the style and fit that is the most effective.

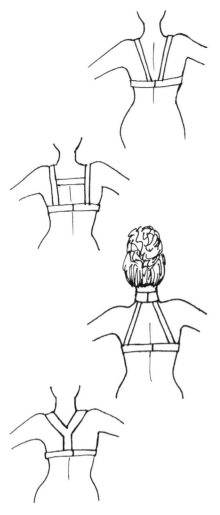

1. The halter style bra will create the maximum cleavage effect, pulling the upper edge of the bra cups inward towards the neck. To minimize neck strain, only use this style for women who need less support and do not pull so tightly as to create strain. Make an opening in the neck strap so that you can open and close it when getting dressed.

2. Standard over-the-shoulder styles work well. However, the straps can sometimes slip. To avoid strap slippage, you can bring your straps in towards the closure at the back. If the straps are already made and you have a slippage problem, attach a piece of elastic, covered and decorated to match, across the upper shoulder region. The elastic will allow enough give during a performance, but will keep the straps on the shoulder.

3. Collar styles are a variation on the halter but the weight is evenly distributed around the entire neck, rather than just focused on the back of the neck. This style can be made filled-in at the chest to create a dramatic design that covers everything.

4. The "Y" style is similar to a sports bra. This style leaves the shoulders free while taking the pressure off of the neck. The "Y" usually comes down the center of the back, so the closure is either under the bottom edge of the strap, which can get bulky, or the closure is moved slightly to the left or the right.

5. Novelty straps can add dramatic lines to the front of your bra, making it look less like lingerie and more like a designer outfit. However, avoid center straps if you have a large bust that needs more support. Multiple thin straps that radiate from a thicker strap on the shoulder can be a very exciting look.

Cleavage

For many dancers, creating cleavage is a challenge. To best optimize or minimize what you have, you have to achieve the perfect fit, the best amount of coverage, and the proper application of padding. To create the ultimate in cleavage, you will want to tilt the cups. This means bringing the underwires down lower so instead of making a "U" shape under the bust, the wire makes a "C" shape around the outside of the bust mound. This is the miraculous secret behind the cleavage-enhancing push-up bras available on the market. Tilting the cups pushes the breasts not only up, but in as well. The tighter the fit, the more cleavage will be created.

Artist rendition of an original design by "Julia."

To create the illusion of even more cleavage, you may want to pad your bra. If you plan on using padding, consider using shoulder pads. It is a good way to recycle. Other options include cotton, foam, batting, fiberfill, and even that old fashioned standby: socks. Many fabric stores, upscale department stores, and specialty lingerie

Bringing the cups together.

Where to place the padding.

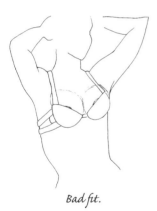

Bad fit.

Good fit.

shops carry specially designed push-up pads that really add a lot of lift. Place your pads the during the fitting process. Do this in front of a mirror so you can evaluate the effect you are creating. Make sure to look from the sides as well as the front.

Pads should be placed to follow the line of the wires. This means that pads should fill in from the sides and the bottom. In the illustration, the hatched marked area represents the area to place the pads. If you want to give the look of a fuller bustline you may want to buy cups that are one size larger than what you would normally wear. Then you will fill in the space with pads from the sides and below. The larger cup will visually expand your chest and give the illusion that there is more of you than is actually there. Make sure to line your bra so your padding doesn't pop out when least expected. You don't want the audience to know that it isn't all you they are seeing. It is your special effect, not theirs.

For a large bust, make sure that your bra provides enough coverage so that you are not oozing out at the sides or at the top and also make sure the straps provide enough support. You may not be able to find a hard-cupped or padded bra in a larger size. However, with the use of good materials and well placed decoration, you can make even the sturdiest support bra look like a million bucks. First, you will not want to cut the cups apart as this will weaken the support structure. Next, cover the outside of the bra with non-stretching materials to support the decorations and avoid stretching out. A strip of grosgrain ribbon should be applied to the edge of your cup to prevent it from stretching further. You can also buy fabric stiffeners to make the cups hard. If you use these products remember that they are water soluble and may break down with sweat and will need to be lined. You will have more spaces to decorate a full bra, but before sewing on a good deal of beaded fringe, consider that these bras usually cannot support great amounts of weight on the cups. Instead, attach fringe to the straps and along the bottom edges.

Straps should be made out of a material that is sturdy and resists stretching. Grosgrain ribbon, belting, and heavy duty interfacing intended for waistlines make good straps. Other materials such as twill tape or nylon webbing work well, too. You will cover your straps to match your costume. Cover the straps before you sew them onto your costume. When you attach your straps, make sure that your stitches are firm and evenly spaced. A lot of stress is placed on the seam between the straps and the cups. Even stitches will spread the stress smoothly throughout the seam. Use a heavy duty button and carpet thread to attach straps. This is one area of the costume you absolutely do not want falling off!

Decorating the Bra

Your imagination is the limit when it comes to the decoration of the bra. There are many different locations on the bra to apply decorations. Below is a list of areas to apply surface details and fringe to bring your bra to life. Remember that the exact same bra and belt base can look entirely different with different decorative schemes.

Fringe: Apply your fringe at the fullest portion of the bust for the most movement. Fringe can be applied horizontally or vertically. They can follow the curve of the face of the bra cups or the bottom edge. The fringe can link the two cups together across the middle, either by stitching it to the center or by spanning the gap without stitching. Fringe can be hung in layers to add color and interest and more movement. Don't forget the area around the back straps.

Appliqués, beaded areas, and decorative stitching: It may be impractical to hang fringe from the tops of the cups or the center piece, so these are areas where you can add other kinds of decorations. Some dancers don't use any fringe on the bra at all, so the entire cup can become the surface for decoration.

Swags of beads: Like fringe, swags add movement to the bra. They can be hung anywhere fringe can be hung, but remember that a swag needs to be attached at both ends, so when designing your swags, make sure you plan for both ends.

Braid and decorative trims: These linear elements can be used to define shapes and to hide the raw and unsightly edges of beaded and fabric trims. These can be used along edges or switched back and forth over an area to cover the surface.

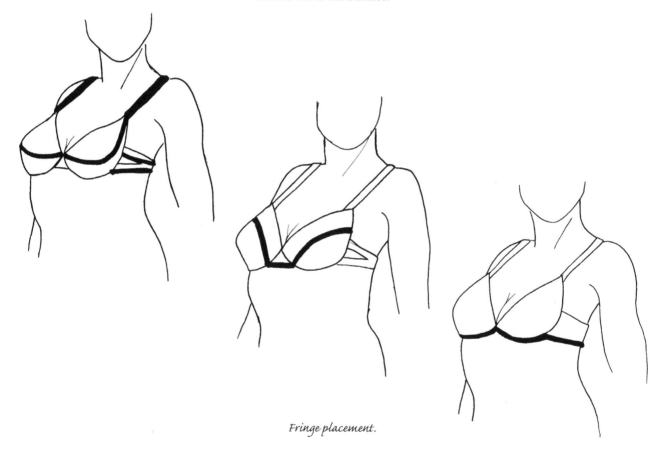

Fringe placement.

5 Leg Coverings

In Middle Eastern Dance the legs do most of the work. In order to maintain the illusion of effortless movement, you will want to cover your legs. There are three ways to cover your legs: a skirt, pants, or a full-length garment. There are numerous variations in skirts and pants to choose from. Remember that these are just a few suggestions. Use your creativity to come up with new costume ideas.

Skirts

Straight Skirt

The straight skirt consists of two rectangular panels that fit the hips snugly. The skirt opens on two sides either over the tops of the thighs or down the sides. Straight skirts need these openings to allow for freedom of movement. During the course of the performances the legs will be in view of the audiences, so be warned: this style is only for those with total confidence in displaying their thighs. However, there are advantages to this style. Straight skirts are very cost-efficient. No fullness is needed, so a minimum amount of yardage is required during construction. More elaborate fabrics and those with body or stiffness adapt well to the straight format.

Straight skirt patterns are simple.

The construction is pretty simple. Two rectangles of fabric are attached to a waistband or casing and then edge-stitched and hemmed. A hook and eye or an elastic band complete the skirt. This type of skirt can be made quickly with a minimum of resources. Many dancers use strips of fabric attached a few inches below their belt to prevent the skirt from flipping up or out and revealing things best left to the imagination. Some professional dancers use fabulously decorated ribbons that allow them not only to display their perfect legs, but creates yet another location for their beautiful beadwork.

The hem of the straight skirt can be modified in a number of different ways. First, the hem can be shaped with fringe or decorative edging applied to accentuate the unusual cut. Second, a ruffle can be added from the knee level or lower, as a single element or in tiers, to add further design interest. Often these ruffles are made from fabrics that constrast in either material or color.

The Sarong

sarong

This variation of the straight skirt combines both of the openings into one spectacular one, usually in the front over the top of one thigh. The same basic principles apply to the creation of the sarong. The big difference is in the final effect—it can be more elegant or more wicked. It also allows the dancer to feature the more attractive leg or side while concealing a less presentable

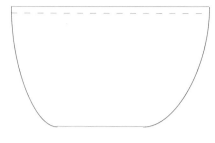

Sarong pattern.

Gathered straight skirt.

Very full circular skirt.

one. This style should be made out of fabric with some give to it. It can, if the fabric is tightly woven, hamper larger lower body movements. If this style is made with fabric containing a mild stretch, the skirt will cling to the buttocks, accentuating this feature.

The graceful asymmetrical sweep of the sarong give the viewer's eye a track to follow up from the feet to the hip area. Visually it will accent the length of the legs and enhance the height of the dancer. Again, the hem need not be straight. It can curve or be cut in an edge pattern to make the garment distinctive.

Gathered Straight Skirt

The gathered straight skirt is designed to add fullness and flow to the total outfit, while minimizing the amount of work needed to produce the costume. The gathered skirt is made using the basic straight skirt concept. This time, though, there is much more fabric, sometimes up to four times the hip measurement. In this style, a casing is required. Merely fold over the top of the fabric and sew to form a casing. Draw the elastic through the casing and pull so it fits firmly around the hips. Finish the hem and edges and trim the garment. If you desire splits in the front, a narrow panel can be added before sewing the casing.

The main advantage to this style is the speed and simplicity with which the garment can be constructed. The fabric, because it is left in essentially one piece, can be used again for another purpose later. In addition, this method is great if you are in a hurry yet require a style with fullness. There are two main disadvantages to this style. First, there is a great deal of bulk at the hipline caused by compressing and gathering the hem. Second, it causes a bell-like silhouette during fast spins or turns.

Circular Skirt

Circular skirts have been used in dance for centuries. They create a smooth, flowing, swirl of fabric that conceals the legs of the dancers. Many performers wear the traditional two-slit variety with more fullness in the back. Most full skirts are made up of three panels—one in front, two in back. A center seam connects the two back panels while the front panel is separated from the back of the skirt allowing the legs to peek through during the dance. More panels can be added to create a more luxurious skirt with more fullness. Typical fabrics include sheer or opaque chiffons, polyester silkies or dress fabric, crepes, pongees, or any other fabrics with a light flowing texture. Fabrics with a crisper texture like lamé, organza, or tulle can be used as well, but with less fullness. The crisper texture will make the fabric stand away from the body and give an appearance of more fullness.

There are three major steps in creating the circular skirt: layout and cutting, construction, and finishing. The standard skirt takes seven to ten yards of fabric, depending on how many panels you desire. When you are choosing fabric make sure it is at least as wide as your hip-to-hem measurement. This measurement is crucial in the layout of the circular skirt. It forms the basic measurement of the pattern. If you plan on making more than one skirt using this method, you may want to create a pattern. Instead of doing the marking on fabric, use paper instead. This way, you will be able to use the same pattern over and over again and skip the layout step in the future.

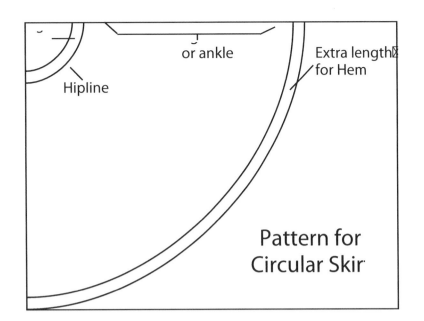

Hipline

or ankle

Extra length
for Hem

Pattern for
Circular Skir

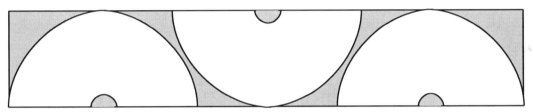

Conserving fabric with circular skirt pieces.

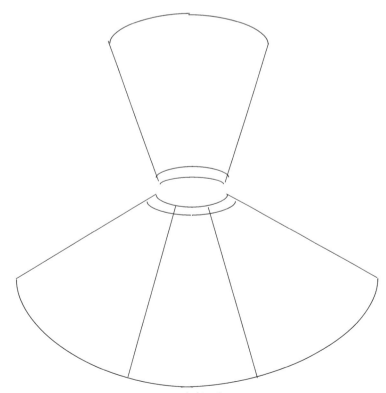

Four-panel skirt layout.

Cutting Directions

1. Begin by taking the measurement from the hip line (at the height you prefer) to just below the ankle.

2. Add three inches (8 cm) to this measurement: one inch (3 cm) at the top where you will attach the skirt to the hip band, and two inches (5 cm) at the bottom for the hem.

3. Take a string or measuring tape and mark this total length plus 4" (10 cm). This extra bit allows for the circular cutout at the hip line.

4. Lay out your fabric, folding it so that the length is equal to the length of your string. You can save time by making several layers of fabric and cutting out all of your semicircles at once. Be sure to pin through all layers of fabric before cutting.

5. Pin the end of your string to the corner at the fold.

6. Swing the string in an arc from one edge of the fabric to the other. As you go, mark the cutting edge on your fabric using chalk, pins, or a erasable fabric pen. Mark the four-inch cutout at the top as well.

7. Unpin the string and cut through all layers of the fabric. When you are done you should have one or more half-circles with a smaller half-circle in the center.

Sewing Directions

Once you have cut out your skirt panels, you get to choose your waist-band style.

Self casing: In this method the hipline edge is folded over and stitched down to create a tube wide enough to slip the elastic through.

Attached casing: In this method a separate length of fabric is attached to the skirt panels. This method is nice because you can use pre-folded bias tape or blanket binding to save some time.

Yoke: This method is good when there is a great deal of fabric at the hip line. For extremely full skirts, a yoke will cut down on the amount of fabric under the belt. Cut a front and back piece out of the same fabric. This piece should reach around the hips comfortably with a bit of extra to spare. The top edge is turned under as in the self casing and the skirt panels are sewn onto the lower edge.

After you have sewn your skirt together and drawn elastic through the waistline, hang your skirt up for a few days. This will allow the fabric to stretch along the bias. You will notice that after a few days, the hem line will be crooked or wavy. Re-draw the hem line onto the fabric to even out the hem. Finish the edge and add some trim.

Tiered Skirts

Another popular style is the tiered skirt. There are two basic types of tiers. In one, the tiers are stitched together to create a very full skirt at the hem line. The other style is to attach tiers to a base skirt like giant ruffles.

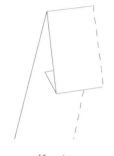

self casing.

Attached casing.

Yoke with fold line for casing.

The first style of tired skirt is constructed from long strips of gathered fabric. This style of skirt can be very time-consuming to make. With patience, the results can be fabulous. First decide how many tiers you would like. Three tiers seem standard, although I have seen fabulous skirts with just one tier added. Remember, the more tiers, the more sewing you will have to do.

1. Determine the number of tiers in the skirt. Divide your hip-to-ankle (or hip-to-floor) measurement by the number of tiers. For our sample, we will use a hip-to-floor length of 38" and we will design three tiers. $38 \div 3 = 12.66$. Round this number up or down to the nearest half or whole inch. We'll use 12.5" as the height of our bands. Add the seam allowance you prefer. For the purposes of this demo, I will add half an inch to each side for a total depth of 13.5".

2. Determine the amount of fullness you would like at the hem. This can be an arbitrary number such as six yards, ten yards, or even twelve yards of fabric. Then you need to determine how gathered you want it. Most skirts are a minimum of 2:1 gathering, which means for every one inch on the middle tier there are two inches on the lower tier. So for a 2:1 skirt, the bottom tier is ten yards, the middle tier is five yards and the top tier is 2.5 yards

3. Is there a directional pattern on your fabric? If the fabric has a horizontal pattern or no pattern, proceed to the next step. If there is a pattern to the fabric, you will need to cut and sew a lot of little pieces to achieve a wide circumference. Divide your desired circumference by the width of the fabric to determine how many panels you will need to stitch together for the lowest tier. So, if the fabric width is 45", what will we need? Change your ten yards to inches, 360", and divide by 45" to find out that you will need eight panels for your lowest tier. Using the ratios from the previous stem, this means that you will need four panels for your middle tier and two for your top tier.

4. If there is no directional pattern, you can lay out your tiers in any way that is convenient to you. You can buy ten yards for a tier unbroken by seams. On 45" wide fabric, we can mark out our tiers without piecing and have enough left over to make a matching vest or choli. You can draw your cutting lines right on the fabric with an erasable pen or chalk.

5. Finish the hem and, if you can, serge the edges now before construction begins. This will save a lot of time later.

Gathering stitch: zigzag over central thread or dental floss.

6. Mark your gathering edge every two feet. Mark your ungathered edge every foot. These markings will allow you to arrange your gathers evenly. To gather the fabric you can run gathering stitches, set at the widest stitch length possible on your machine, along the gathering edge. You will want at least three rows of gathering stitches so that if one breaks, you still have two to work with. An alternative method is to zig-zag over a piece of heavy weight thread or dental floss and pull that up.

7. Gather until your marks line up. Pin the gathered edge to the next tiers ungathered edge and stitch.

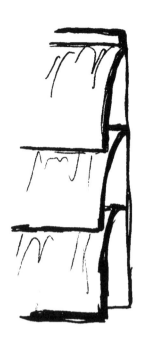

8. Complete your garment by adding a casing and running elastic through or attaching a fitted hip band.

Remember not all of your tiers have to match or be made out of the same fabric. However, try to get the fabrics to be of similar weights or, if they are not, make the lowest tier from the lightest weight fabric.

For a tiered skirt where the tiers are loose, create a base skirt either by using the circle skirt pattern and making two panels, one front and one back, or by using the gathered straight or straight skirt layout. To calculate the depth of your tiers, divide your hip-to-hem (or hip-to-floor) measurement by the number of tiers you want. For a sample, we want three tiers and our measurement is 38"; 38" ÷ 3 = 12.66". Now, because you don't want to see your stitch lines, we will increase the depth by several inches. In our case, we will increase the tiers by three inches, plus one more for seam allowance, and round up to the nearest whole inch, taking our total to 17". Your top tier will not have the additional three inches added, so the top tier is only 14".

On the base skirt, mark rows for your tiers by dividing the space evenly, or every 12.5 inches. This is where the bottom of each tier will land. Now measure these rows and multiply by 2 or 3 for the length of your tier. Gather using the directions above and then pin the tiers on so that the bottom edges line up with the markings. Attach the top at the hip line. Attach the second one so that the edge matches the line of the base tier and attach the base tier so that the bottom edge lines up with the hem.

This sounds really complicated, but if you look at the illustration to the left, you will see how this is created and what results are. Making tiered skirts can be very time-consuming and takes up more fabric than other styles, but the results can be wonderful!

Overskirt Ideas

Overskirts of all shapes and lengths can be made to add variety to your costume wardrobe. The handkerchief-hemmed skirt is one example. In this skirt, a square of fabric is used. Fold the fabric in half, and in half again. Draw a curve four inches down from the folded corner. This is your hip line. The length of the skirt is from the hip line to the corner. Finish the hipline using a casing or yoke. These types of skirts can be worn alone if long enough, with pants, or over a full skirt.

A very simple overskirt style is to create two elaborately trimmed panels that hang in front and back over a fuller skirt. Because they are relatively small, they can be a cost-efficient manner for utilizing a very expensive piece of fabric. Decorate the edges and either pin to the belt or pin to the top of the skirt. They can also be attached to a narrow band and worn as a separate piece.

Pants

Pants are a very useful costume element. They can be layered under combinations or skirts, for example. The modest dancer or the performer who wants to hide unsightly scars may choose to wear pants. Some dancers wear pants that are cut with a lot of fullness without a skirt or combination above. Pants free the dancer from worry about what may or may not show. As

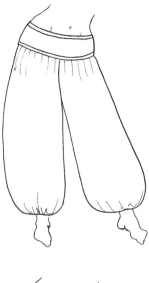

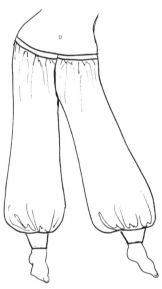

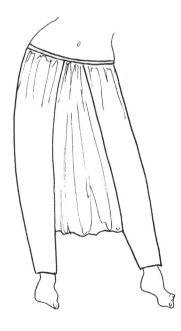

long as the pants are full enough to allow total freedom of movement, they are a suitable costume option for any type of dancer. There are many subtle variations possible. However, there are only two basic styles: harem pants and Turkish pants.

Harem Pants

Harem pants are an ancient loose-fitting garment consisting of two panels which are gathered at the waist and ankles. The variations in this style occur in the width of the pant legs and in the height of the hip line. The key to remember is to make them at least two inches wider than your widest measurement to ensure they will fit.

Adapt an existing pattern to create harem pants. Sweat pants are just a more closely-fitted version of harem pants. Purchase a sweat pants pattern and lower the hip line. Add some length and width at the bottom of the leg and you have the basic harem pants pattern. Be sure to test your altered pattern in sample fabric before making it out of expensive material.

For traditional harem pants made entirely from rectangles, a gusset will be needed to allow room for the crotch and to make sitting and moving possible. First make two rectangles the length of your leg from hip to ankle. Make them any width you desire to achieve the fullness you have designed. You will want to make your gusset at least 5" (13 cm) square; a larger gusset means more comfort and anything less will prevent movement. Most of the garments I make have a gusset of at least 10 inches (25 cm).

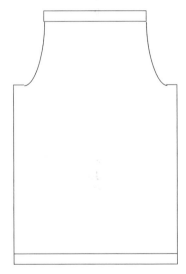

Harem pants pattern.

1. Create a rectangle from your hip-to-ankle measurement. Add 3 inches (8 cm) to top and bottom for casings. Mark the crotch length for your pants from your hip down. Put this mark on all four edges of your pants pattern.

2. Attach the gusset from this mark down on one side of the pants.

3 Pin the leg closed all the way up to the crotch length mark. This means switching from the leg to the gusset at the top.

4. Now take the second leg and pin the third side of the gusset to the leg and stitch it down. Repeat step three with the second leg.

5. Turn the legs inside out and line up the front seam and back seam. The bottom of the crotch curve has been created by the gusset, so stitch down to where the gusset begins and reinforce the area well with back stitching.

6. When you look down into the pants the gusset should look like the illustration.

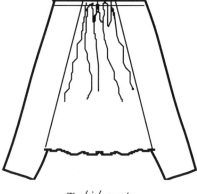

Turkish pants

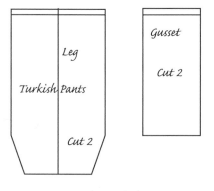

Pattern for Turkish pants

Harem pants can be made more revealing by cutting a slit up the side of the leg. This slit will allow the viewer flashes of leg during the performance. If you slit the leg be sure to finish the edge and reinforce the top and bottom of the slit. You can add a yoke to the top to reduce bulk under the hip region and add decorative cuffs at the bottom. Combine elements to create the pants that are the most flattering, then save the pattern and use it over and over again.

Turkish Pants

Turkish pants are very popular today in parts of North Africa and throughout the Middle East. This style is very comfortable because it allows the wearer to move easily and without restriction. This is due to the large gusset down the middle of the pants. Follow the directions below to make a pattern for the Turkish pants.

1. Collect all of the tools you will need to create the pattern. This includes: ruler, tape measure, colored pencils, square, and large paper.

2. Draw out two rectangles. One should be double the measure from your hip to your knee by the desired width of the gusset (between ten and twenty inches, or 25–50 cm). The second rectangle should be the length of the pants from hip to ankle by the width of the calf plus 10 inches (25 cm). Add length to both of these pieces for the hip casing.

3. Take the second rectangle and measure up from ankle to the knee. On the bottom line, mark the calf measurement plus 1" (3 cm). Make sure you center this in the middle of the paper. From the knee, draw an angle down and inward to the bottom at the ends of the calf line.

4. Add seam allowance to all pieces.

5. Stitch the garment together by sewing the pant legs up to where the gusset will start. Then pin in the gusset and stitch all the way around one leg, and then the other. Make a casing at the top and run cord or elastic through.

After you have created the pattern, test it by making a sample pair of pants. If you make any adjustments, transfer these to the pattern. When you put the pants together, sew from the calf up to the knee measurement, then attach the gusset to each leg. Sew the casing and run elastic through it to finish the top of the pants.

Turkish pants with decorated cuffs

Slit harem pants with decorative overskirt.

Pants with a Gusset

In preindustrial cultures, garments were made out of whole cloth with no curves or darts. In order to accommodate the body, gussets were added to fit the figure. The directions below will make a pair of loose-fitting pants that are perfect for re-enactors.

1. Cut two large rectangles. The length of each should be equal to the length of your leg plus a few inches for ease and a casing of between five and six inches (13–16 cm). You can make these pants with or without a side seam. If you choose to make them without the side seam, you can skip step 7.

2. Stitch the gusset onto the left front panel at crotch level (with an inch or two for ease).

3. Stitch the left back panel from the hem to the edge of the gusset.

4. Stitch the gusset onto the right front panel, making sure both front panels are on the same side of the gusset.

5. Stitch the right back panel from the hem to the edge of the gusset.

6. Turn the pant's right sides together. Line up and stitch the center front seam and the center back seam.

7. Carefully fold the right leg inside the left and stitch the left outside seam. Repeat for the right by folding up the left leg inside the right.

8. Finish by pressing a casing and stitching. Run cord or elastic through.

On the patterpieces below, seam allowance has been added but is not drawn in. The stitch lines are indicated by dotted lines.

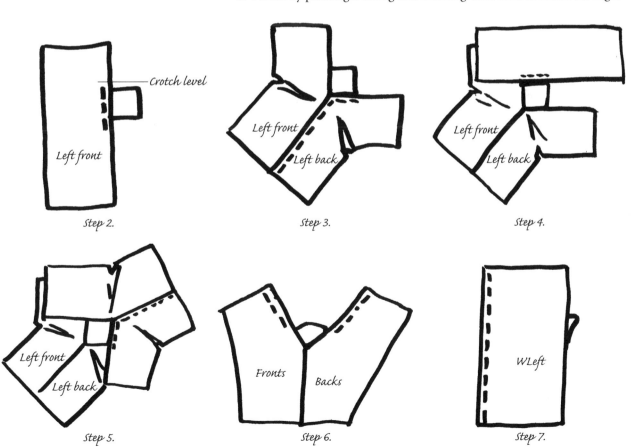

Handkerchief hem overskirt.

6 Combinations

Combinations are full-length garments that extend from the shoulder line to the hem. Variations of many of these styles have been worn by women in the Middle East for centuries. Through choice in fabrics you can make these simple styles rich and exciting.

Turkish Coat

This dress style comes from Turkey and spread throughout the Middle East during the reign of the Ottoman Empire from the fifteenth hrough the nineteenth centuries. Traditionally, these coats were called *anteri* (Turkish for robe) and were worn in layers. Often these were buttoned only through the torso and left open from the waist down. Contrasting prints and solids were created through the layering process. Turkish-styled pants were worn beneath for both comfort and modesty.

A sleeveless version of the anteri was called the *yelek*. Underneath, Turkish women wore a lightweight, even sheer chemise known as a *gömlek*. Both the anteri and the yelek frequently cut below the bust line allowing the gömlek to show at the neck line. Frequently the bust was exposed through the transparent fabric. For modern modesty's sake, the anteri and yelek were often cut higher, to cover the bust line, or worn with a decorative bra for a fusion look.

Images from the nineteenth century depict dancers from Egypt to Turkey wearing variations of this style. Patterns for this style of garment are available through Middle Eastern importers or dance supply houses. A simple pattern can be drafted from the measurements taken in Chapter 1. The best fabric for these fitted garments is one that is firmly woven and sturdy. Brocades and velvets make very sumptuous anteri.

Because of its long history, the anteri is suitable for historical re-creations and is often worn by members of living history groups and Renaissance Fairs. Together with a pillbox-styled cap or turban, harem pants, and a corded sash or scarf, a complete costume can be made from relatively inexpensive materials. Cotton is particularly nice for living history purposes. It is a traditional material that can be readily cleaned. Choose fabrics in colors that reflect dye processes used historically. Traditional colors from naturally occurring dyes include: orange, red, rust, ocher, all shades of brown, blues, greens, yellows, and some purples. For that fully historical look, you may even want to do your own dying with traditional dyestuffs. To get a good idea of what is acceptable for historical garments, look at artworks from Persia, Turkey, India, and Egypt during the period you are re-creating to get a sense of what is authentic and what is not. Keep in mind that, historically, people danced in whatever they happened to be wearing, so look at all garments, not just what was worn by dancers.

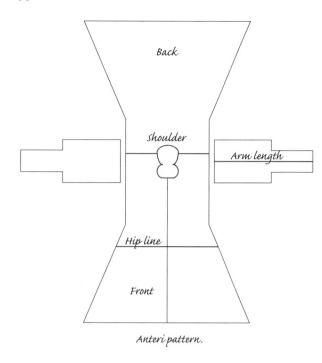

Anteri pattern.

A keyhole-shaped neckline is common although historical images indicate that V-neck and rounded necklines were also popular. Dagged or pointed hem lines also change the look of this garment while maintaining an authentic look. Often the front sides were pulled back from the hem and tucked into the hip band. This would reveal another layer below and would allow the wearer to take full advantage of all of their garments. Layers could be made all the same length, but pulled back to different degrees to allow some layers to show more than others. In addition, this style will make the wearer appear to have a wider variety of garments than would otherwise be evident. Mixing and matching multiple layers of anteri can add a rich and colorful dimension to your dance.

Anteri, like all combinations, have the added benefit of keeping the midriff covered. If you are in the market to cover unsightly bulges or scars, this is one style that is perfect for you. A decorative bra or blouse can be worn beneath anteri, cut below the bustline for a modern twist on the traditional style. Because the anteri closes up the front, decorative buttons can bring this garment to life, adding a focus of color or, with metallic buttons, a jeweled accent. This garment can be made with an inset up the middle that leaves a gap at the waist and at the chest level. This inset will allow for weight loss as well as adding another dimension to the plain design. If you have an older anteri that no longer fits, you can add an inset to bring it up to size without compromising the lines of the garment.

Before making the final garment, you may want to make a sample to identify needed alterations or changes to the pattern.

1. Using a yardstick and a pencil, draw a rectangle as wide as your shoulders and as long as *twice* your shoulder-to-floor measurement.

2. Measure down to your waist and draw a line on both the front and back. Then draw your hip line on the front and back. If the waist line is too large, you may want to shape in a curve. If the waist measurement is too narrow, you may want to add shaped side panels. To calculate the width of each side panel, subtract the total length from your waist measurement, add 2" (5 cm) to the difference and divide by four. Do the same calculation at the hip. Mark the addition for the hip and for the waist and then draw an angled line to the hem line.

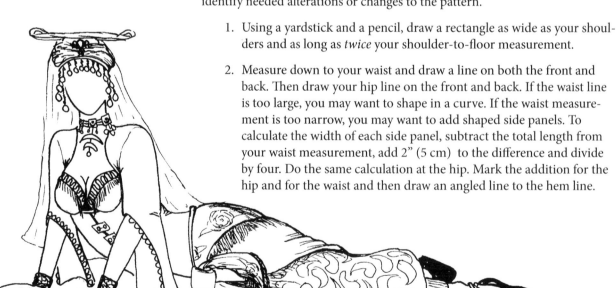

Kaftan with embroidered panels.

3. Decide how you will close the garment. If you want the edges to just line up, you can use buttons and loops or decorative frogs. If you add an inch, you can have the fronts overlap like a shirt and put in buttons and button holes.

4. If you are making an anteri, use your arm length to create the sleeve. The sleeve width should be equal to your bicep measurement plus and inch or two of ease. If you want really wide sleeves, make this measurement bigger. Draw a straight line equal to your arm length, then mark your wrist measurement, again with ease added for comfort and motion range.

5. Make a diamond-shaped gusset 5 or 6 inches (13–15 cm) long. This will be sewn into the sleeve and side seams and will allow a greater range of motion. You may want to first experiment with sewing in gussets on inexpensive fabrics before moving onto more expensive garments.

6. Stitch the garment together. Attach the side panels and sew on the sleeves and gussets.

As with any garment, there are variations that can be made to the anteri for variety. You can leave slits open along the seams below the hip line. The side seams can be laced shut, as can the front. The sleeves can be finished with buttons and loops, rather than stitching up the entire sleeve, allowing them to be worn open or closed. Look at pictures until you find the design elements that you wish to emulate and create the look that is entirely your own.

Kaftan

The traditional dress worn by men and women, the ka*ftan* is a staple of Middle Eastern dress from across the Middle East and North Africa. Kaftans come in an amazing range of widths, colors, and fabrics. They can be as loose as the *thobe* from Arabia or as tight as the severely straight styles from Palestine. Kaftans can also be made shorter and worn with pants. This is especially comfortable during performances of Debke, which requires the dancer to sink low to the ground and bounce up frequently.

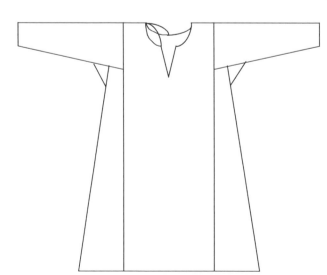

Traditional kaftans were constructed out of narrow lengths of cloth. Bedouin women used narrow portable looms that dictated the maximum width for their cloth. Most averaged in width from 20" to 30" (50–75 cm). The center portion of the kaftan was cut as one piece with the neck opening at the center. The arms were tapered rectangles that were attached to the middle of the center length. Extra fabric cut in triangular shapes was added to create the desired fullness. A gusset was added to allow for maximum movement of the arms.

The directions for creating a kaftan are similar to the anteri, except the kaftan traditionally has a much narrower hem and does not open up the front. Instead, it has a slit down the front from the neckline that allows for the wearing of the garment. Contemporary kaftans are cut in

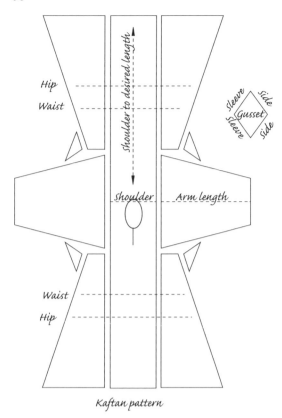

Kaftan pattern

a single body piece due to the availability of textiles in wider widths. In addition, arms are often set into shaped arm holes eliminating the need for the traditional gusset. Sometimes these modern elements are combined to create new looks. The gallabia is the men's version of the kaftan. Like the kaftan, it is a long, loose-fitting garment. However, from the waist up it looks like a contemporary Western-styled shirt.

1. Begin by making a rectangle the width of your shoulders plus 2" (5 cm) by the length from your shoulders to your ankles. Make sure that this is enough fabric to reach around the hip area. Either a) add width to the bottom of the rectangle and angle the sides out to meet this new width or b) determine the width you desire for the hem line and create triangular side pieces to extend the width.

2. Draw in your neckline.

3. Create a gusset approximately 5" (13 cm) long in a diamond format.

4. Create a sleeve by beginning with a rectangle the length of your arm and width of your biceps measurement plus 2" to 5". Extend the wrist line and redraw the sides.

Use this layout as a guide. As long as you use your measurements as a base and add onto them to change the style, the costume should fit. You will probably want two or three extra inches around your abdomen so that you will have plenty of space when performing stomach rolls. Sew the sleeves to the body. Add gussets and stitch the sides. Hem and trim as desired.

The Thobe

The *thobe* is an Arabian kaftan of expanded proportions. Worn as an outer garment, the thobe makes a beautiful cover-up or dance costume, especially when performing the Kalegee. With long flowing lines, the thobe takes up a lot of fabric but has the benefit of hiding everything. It can be made of a sheer fabric such as a chiffon and worn over a bra and belt for a more modest display of finery.

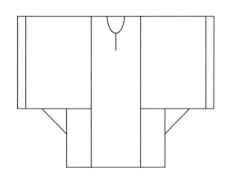

Like the kaftan, the thobe was traditionally made from narrow lengths of cloth. It also possesses gussets, even though it does not need them to allow for freedom of movement. The thobe has large arm openings that are essential for desert wear. These openings cool the wearer by allowing the air to circulate through the garment.

The thobe is made in the same way the kaftan is, except the pattern pieces are all widened. Do not add length to the sleeve or your hands will disappear and it will become difficult to perform. To stitch up the garment, sew each entire side section together and then attach them to the central panel. Use decorative stitching and embroidery to decorate the surface of the garment.

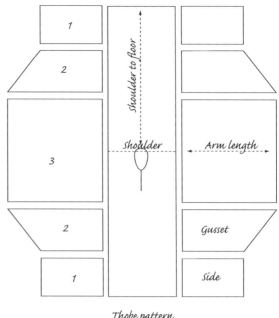

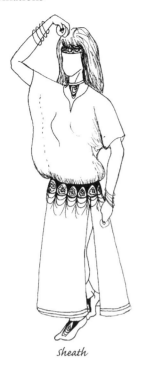

Thobe pattern

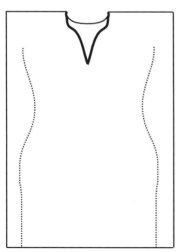

Sheath

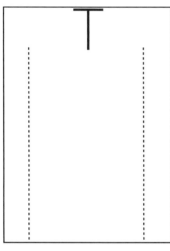

Sheath

The sheath is the epitome of simplistic design. Quite simply, it is a tube or fold of fabric that is stitched up the sides. With a minimum amount of work this style can be fashioned out of the most sumptuous fabrics, or it can be made out of plain cloth and embellished with surface decorations. The sheath is nice for its ability to be as form-fitting as you like, or as loose and flowing as you can maneuver in.

For this style all you need are two basic measurements: your height and your arm span. Remember your other dimensions as well. The sheath must be able to slip over your entire body. What this means is that it should be no less than 2" (5 cm) wider than your widest measurement. Let me give you an example. If my hips measure 40" then the smallest the sheath can be is 42". This is a very tight fit! You may want to curve your seam slightly to fit your contours. Make the sheath to fit your moves. If you raise your arms over your head, allow some extra length so that you can get them up there. As your shoulders go up, so does your costume. When you tie a scarf or belt around the hips, make sure there is a little bit of extra length so that your movements will not be impeded.

There are many possibilities for the sheath. It can be made of shiny glitzy cabaret fabric, or simple cottons for a more historic look. Rows of fringe or pailettes will turn a simple sheath into a shimmy dress. Several sheath dresses can be worn piled one on top of another to achieve the look of the Ouled Nail dancers. Add piles of jewelry and braided wigs with more jewelry in the hair for the total effect. Be creative and use what you have to make your costume the best it can be.

Ouled Nail

Beladi Dress

Many dancers prefer a more tailored look than a simple sheath. For those who are interested in complete coverage while accentuating the lines of the body, a fitted beladi dress is for you. These dresses can be purchased from most dancewear vendors, as the most elaborate can be time-consuming to make. Some are constructed with a built-in bra, others are made out of spandex and are designed to fit snugly around the body. These dresses are often trimmed like a cabaret outfit in sequins, pailettes, and beads, but they can be made of natural fibers for a more historically-inspired garment. Variations of the simple beladi dress can be found in Orientalist paintings of the nineteenth century.

I recommend that if you are thinking of making a beladi dress, go to your local fabric store and find a pattern for an evening dress that you really like and use it as a basis for your dress. These patterns will have the fitted darts and perhaps even some design features that will make the transition into belly dancewear easy. Some dancers begin with a leotard and add scarves to the bottom edge to create a beladi dress style that fits like a second skin.

Again, when designing this type of garment, change the hem line, the sleeves, and the neckline to personalize the garment and make it your own.

Beladi dress.

The same outfit will look different with changes in materials, neckline, and sleeves

Fibula

Wrapped Garments

Across North Africa many women wear wrapped garments that are based on the garments of the Greeks and Romans. In Morocco, women wear the *haik,* which is a garment that wraps around the body several times and even over the head. It is held together by a pair of *fibula,* or pins at the shoulders. In Tunisia, a similar garment is the Mi'laya, which is also wrapped around the body and held in place by fibula. Many performers have their own interpretations of these traditional garments. The format for wrapping varies according to region and purpose.

Most wrapped garments are made of fabric that is as wide as the wearer's shoulder height. The wrapping process begins at the front of the body, wrapping to the back where it is pulled over the shoulders and pinned to the front. The wrapping can continue once or twice more, often with a long end being left free to cover the head. This style is worn during performances of the Guedra with long braids elaborately formed on the head, wrapped with jewelry, beads, shells, and other decorative items.

Algerian dancer.

Guedra.

Designing for Every Body

Many people are concerned about the proportions of their figure—feeling their legs are too heavy, their breasts too large or too small, or their arms too flabby to wear bedleh. However, there are features which can be designed into costumes to create a beautiful ensemble emphasizing their body's best attributes and minimizing perceived problems. Starting from the top down, I am going to list a number of design suggestions for visually concealing, enhancing, and reshaping the body. Most of these design elements are geared for cabaret-styled ensembles, but some of the suggestions apply to fusion or folkloric styles as well.

One of the things I suggest to all of my clients before we work together on a costume is to look at themselves in a full length mirror in a dark leotard and leggings. This gives them an idea of the shape of their body without focusing on the details. Every body is different. Knowing what they have to work with allows them to pick features to enhance, reveal, or conceal.

Have a friend take pictures of you in your leotard from the front, back, side, and at a few other different angles. Take these pictures to a copy center and enlarge them, trace them, and then use them as your own personal croquis. Literally draw your costumes onto your body and see what happens. Play with design elements until you find something you love.

Many of these suggestions are features found in a wide variety of costumes. As a designer you can mix and match ideas, tying them together with color, design motifs, and fabrics that coordinate and match. We are going to start from the top down.

Flat, Limp, or Short Hair

- Wigs, hair falls, and hair pieces can cover, blend, and extend your hair, add volume, or even entirely change your look. Make sure you practice dancing in your wig, hair fall, or hair piece so you know what movements to avoid that might dislodge your new hair. You may want to discuss with a professional hairdresser the best way to wear your new hair, style it, and care for it.

- Turbans can be a delightful way to cover your hair. They make the issue of hair unimportant by covering it up. Turbans can be made of the most glittery, exotic fabrics to match a cabaret ensemble and are essential to enhance a historic, folkloric, or tribal costume. Remember, jewels can be pinned to a turban to make it more exotic and beautiful.

- Head cloths can cover hair very simply. A hat or turban can be added to the head cloth to enhance the height of the headdress.

- If you hair is smooth and flat and you want to add height, use a pill box hat. These can be purchased ready-made and covered with your own fabric, or can be constructed from scratch to match your costume. Pill box hats go well with cabaret and folkloric costumes.

- Pull your hair back under a decorative headband an let it fall smoothly over your head. The headband will focus attention at the front. Put jewelry, appliqués, embroidery, or beadwork to match your bra onto the headband to tie your ensemble together.

Short Neck

- Wear necklaces that hang below the collarbone to extend the visual length of the neck. Or, wear no necklace at all, and focus your jewelry scheme on your wrists and ears.

- Avoid wide chokers or collars. They should be made narrow to create the illusion that there is more length there.

- Wear a chest piece that extends from the collar to below the breast. This ties the neck and chest area together. This works really well with Egyptian-style beaded collars creating a pharonic look, but other styles can be achieved.

Narrow Shoulders

- Epaulettes attached to the bra straps can add visual width to the shoulder area and balance out wider hips. Hanging fringe from the epaulettes will add movement and pull the eye to the expanded shoulder region.

- Fringed upper arm drapes can be attached to the bra straps to visually expand this area. These can be dropped from the side of the bra cups or from any space along the bra straps. Experiment in front of a mirror to find the most flattering styles.

- Sleeves attached to either the bra or vest, or worn as separate units, will also add fullness to the shoulder region. Sleeves can be made out of strings of beads as well as fabric, so experiment with different materials until you find a design that you like.

- A vest with stiffened shoulder lines will extend the garment slightly past the edge of the shoulder. Add decorative detail at shoulder line, such as tassels, fringe, or beading. You can add sleeves for more visual interest under the applied designs.

Full Upper Arms

- Wear sleeves, either attached to a garment or as separate sleeves, or puffs to cover and conceal the biceps region. The fabric can be very sheer, or it can be split to show glimpses of your upper arm area. Strings of beads can also be used instead of fabric for this application.

- Use fringed drapes that extend from the straps of the bra to provide camouflage for the upper arm area. See above comments.

- Wear a dress with sleeves, a caftan, thobe, or anteri. These combination garments usually have sleeves and can hide a multitude of sins.

- Vests or cholis can be made with long sleeves that either match the vest material but can also be made of contrasting fabrics.

- Purchase jewelry and wear cuffs at your biceps if you can. If you have larger arms, make cuffs and decorate to complement your costume. Use the same directions as for wrist cuffs. Make them wide enough to cover the entire offending area or you may inadvertently draw the wrong kind of attention to it.

Small Bust

- Use interesting, asymmetrical, or unusual strap formations. Because you do not have the type of weight-bearing issues larger busted dancers have to deal with, you have greater opportunities to play with strap placement.

- Wear garments that cover the cleavage, such as solid halter tops or ethnic styles that are more covered.

- A vest can be worn over a bra to make a frame for the bustline and add visual bulk to the area. You can enhance this by wearing a gathered shirt across the bust.

Large Bust

- Decorate your wide straps to match your bra and belt. Integrate this surface into your designs. Consider straps another surface for decoration.

- Fit is absolutely important. If you are bulging above your bra cups, use larger cups. You may need more coverage and the bra may not be able to plunge so far. If you use a support bra, decorate it like you would a regular costume bra. Integrate the middle support structure into your design, plan for it, and use it to your advantage.

- Avoid adding bulk to the upper arm region. Use sleek, form-fitting sleeves, Wnot puffs. Don't extend drapes from the straps over the upper arms. Wear decorated gauntlets or cuffs to draw attention to the forearm and wrist area.

- You may want to limit the amount of fringe hanging from the apex of the bust. Use fringe sparingly to avoid looking like a wall of fringe. Break the expanse visually by using larger design elements, or more design elements over the cups of the bra.

Large Ribs, Protruding Abdomen, or Scarring

- Use stomach drapes from the lower edge of the bra to add visual interest and coverage to this area. Stomach drapes can be as simple as a few chains, or as complex as a series of necklaces.

- Hang beaded fringe from the apex of the bust so it swings freely away from the stomach region and make it longer so it covers more. Closely space the beads so that there is less showing through.

- Wear a body stocking, body suit, or a stomach covering that goes from the bottom of the bra to the belt. This can be form-fitting or loose, opaque or semi-sheer, and should either match your skin tone or your costume.

- Wear a combination garment, beladi dress, caftan, thobe, sheath, or anteri. These garments will cover this entire region.

- Learn to do amazing movements in spite of your size. Many dancers who are larger through the middle can accomplish more dramatic stomach rolls and flutters. Audiences are more likely to appreciate a larger stomach region if it can do incredible things.

- If you have stretch marks or surgical scars on the abdomen, you can try cutting your hip belt to conceal your scars. If they are extensive, or spread further up the torso, you can wear a body stocking or stomach drape for fuller coverage.

Wide Hips

- Use more decoration at the center of the belt. Use solid, dark colored, non-shiny fabrics over the hips.

- Do not tuck scarves, tassels, or any other additional fabric items in at the hips.

- Use fringe in the center of the belts, hanging in a "V" shape rather than straight across.

- Cut the top of the belt in a decorative manner, in a "V" or other complex shape, rather than a straight horizontal line.

- Do not pad your belt. Use the minimum amount of stabilizing materials to create a thinner, sleeker line through the hip region.

- Avoid wide swages of beads or chain that reach around the hip region. Keep hanging decorations to the center front and center back portions of the belt.

- Make sure the belt fits well. Avoid really tight belts that make the flesh bulge above, further accentuating the width. Make sure your belt isn't too loose, so it doesn't twist around the body during performances.

Narrow Hips/Little Waist Definition

- Add decoration to the hip area, bring skirts up and tuck them, and/or add scarves to visually increase the width of the hips.

- Pad the belt to add bulk to accentuate the shape of the hip line.

- Wear a combination with vertical stripes, adding fullness at and below the hips. The angled lines will give the illusion of wider hips.

- Use straight cut belts with horizontal lines in the design motifs and in the hang of the beads.

Thick, Heavy, or Veined Legs

- Wear leggings or other opaque hosiery.

- Wear a skirt without slits. Or wear multiple layers of skirts with the slits not lined up so the skirt does not fall open to show the legs.

- Choose to wear pants under a full slit skirt or with an ethnic outfit. There are many pants options that can enhance a garment. Make them out of semi-sheer fabric to give the illusion of seeing more.

- Make dresses with shorter slits up the sides. Control slits with decorative banding that gives the illusion of seeing more than you are actually showing.

- Design a costume around pants as the focal point, so you don't look like you are intentionally covering your legs. Use a half skirt to frame your pants.

- Avoid straight styles if you are uncomfortable with your thighs. Wearing a full skirt can cover a multitude of physical sins.

Above and below: accentuating the hips.

Shorter Frame

- Keep to one uniform color throughout out your entire garment.

- Wear straight skirts and avoid garments that puff away from the body.

- Avoid straight horizontal lines. Wear angles and hang beads in "V" shapes at the shoulder, bust and hip line.

- Wear a vertical hair style or add a headdress for height and make it the same color as the rest of the garment.

- Avoid long stomach drapes, shorten the hang of beaded trim from the bust. Visually lengthen the stomach region by wearing the bra as high as possible and the belt as low as can go.

Tall frame

- Play up your best features any way you like.

- Visually break up your frame with design lines that cut across the body. Beladi dresses with angled lines in the design will look dramatic.

- Don't wear one color head to toe.

- Don't wear shoes that add height. Reduce the height of hair or headdress.

- If you are thin, add more visual interest to the chest and hip areas to increase visual bulk, and draw attention to these areas.

- If you have a long torso, experiment with complex stomach drapes and dramatic long fringe from the bustline.

Heavy Frame

- Wear combination garments that drop from the shoulder in one smooth line. These garments should be fitted and skim the body. If these are worn too tight, it will further draw attention to a heavy frame.

- Focus attention at the center of the body through the use of design motifs, embroidery, and decoration.

- Also focus attention on the face and chest region by emphasizing them with high contrasts in either color, like gold/black, or texture, shiny/matte for example.

- For bedleh, drop your fringe to the edge of your hip belt, hanging them from the fullest portion of the bust, so that they swing free. People will only be able to guess what is underneath, as long as no deep back bends are performed.

- Wear sleeves that are more fitted. Avoid adding puffs and further expanding the figure.

- Wear fitted or straight sleeves to avoid adding additional bulk to the body.

B. CRITES

8 Veils

Veils are the most useful prop the dancer has at her disposal. Many people come to a performance with expectations of what a dancer is supposed to look like or what she will do. For most, a Middle Eastern dancer is expected to wield her veil in slow and sensuous motions during the slow *taxim* portion of her dance. There are several ways to incorporate a veil into the overall scheme of the costume. Many dancers use veils made out of the same fabric as their skirt for a visually unified look. Some dancers buy or make one outstanding veil in a neutral color, such as gold, silver, black, or red. Another option is to buy a multicolored veil to accentuate a wide number of costumes.

There are as many variations of veil technique as there are dancers. However, there are three main types of veils used: rectangular veils, circular veils, and capes. These different shapes allow for variations in veil technique and in choice of materials. There are many sources for wonderful veils decorated in a variety of ways to accentuate any costume. Check the list of vendors in the appendix for sources of beautiful veils.

Rectangular

The rectangular veil is the standard shape used by dancers everywhere. This shape allows for great variation in the initial wrap. Many dancers use their veil as a cover during the opening sections of their routine. During the taxim the dancer will remove her veil, uncovering her body with tantalizing slowness. There are an infinite number of subtle variations on the veil wrap. The look of the wrap will depend upon the length of the veil and what the fabric it is made of.

Veils of this shape can be made out of a wide variety of materials including, but not limited to, chiffon, lace, lightweight knits, crepes, lamés, quianas, lightweight cottons, satins, and silky polyesters. If performances take place outside, a heavier weight veil, made of cotton, brocade, linen, or crepe back satin, among others, will help the dancer keep control during windy situations. The key to determining the type of fabric used is how it drapes and flows through the air. To test this you can try flipping a length around in the fabric store to see if it moves in the manner you like. Cut the fabric to the length you desire and hem it. Trim the edges with braid, ribbon, sequins, fringe, palettes, or coins. Make sure the decoration you

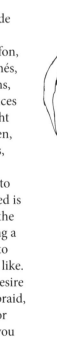

put on the edge doesn't weigh the veil down preventing you from moving it smoothly around your body. Be aware that sequin trim can catch on your hair; make sure to practice at home before taking a new veil into public. Remember, each veil has its own personality!

The rectangular veil varies in size according to taste. The standard is 2 $^1/_2$ to 3 yards long by 45" to 60" wide (2.5–3.0 by 1.5–2.0 meters). The key is to think of your arm span. You want it to be longer by about a foot (0.3 meters) on either side. If you can, experiment with veils owned by friends or instructors to see what types of fabrics you prefer and what size is ideal for you. Some dancers perform with veils that are significantly longer than the above recommended lengths. Experiment to find what works best for you.

Circular

Circular veils can be used in many of the same ways as the rectangular veils, yet there are moves that can only be done with the circular veil that make it swirl and flip like a Matador's cape. During a spin, the circular veil possesses a mind of its own, moving in arcs through space. This type of veil is especially suitable for fabrics that have a little more body and texture than would be used in a rectangular version. They can be stiffer and less inclined to drape than the rectangular veil and still be used with great flair. Some dancers even use two circular veils at the same time to create geometric shapes through the air. Tissue lamé is widely used for double veils, often of two different colors, to create different patterns in the air.

B. CRITES

The circular veil can vary in size from two to three yards (meters) along the straight edge. The pattern is laid out in much the same way you would make a circular skirt. Fold the fabric in half and take a string equal to half of the desired length. Pin it to the corner of the fold and move the string in an arc around the fabric, marking the edge as you go. Cut out this curve and unfold for the final look. Make sure that you do not pull on the fabric when you hem this type of veil; the curve can become distorted with too much pressure. Use a narrow hem rolled by hand, sewing machine, or serger. Edge the hem with any decorative ribbon, braid, sequins, or fringe for a decorative finish. The added weight of the decoration will affect the way the veil handles, so practice.

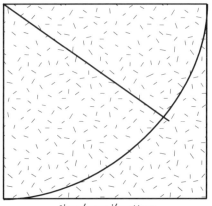

Circular veil pattern.

Capes

A popular variation on the circular veil is the cape. Capes are large versions of the circular veil. However, unlike veils, many capes are designed with neck and arm holes cut into the fabric. Capes are worn in during the entrance and are removed during the course of the performance. Capes often have shaped hems that coordinate or accentuate the garment. The length is a matter of personal preference. They can be short, ending at the hip or knee, or longer, reaching the ankle, skirt hem, or floor. Most pattern companies carry a pattern for a cape. Invest in a pattern for a full cape and cut it down to suit your needs. This is faster than drawing out your own cape and it usually has the correct neck shape already in place.

Where the arm holes are placed is a matter of personal preference and style. A key to remember is the measurement from the neck to the shoulder. Make sure that this is the length between your cape neckline and the top of your arm hole. Because there may be stress on the arm holes during cape removal, be sure to reinforce the top and bottom of the arm openings.

Trim the cape in the same manner you would trim a circular veil. The hem of a cape is much longer, so limit the amount of weight along the edge. Keep in mind that this is a larger costume element and check out the location you will be performing in to prevent any damage to you, your costume, or anything else that might get in the way. Ruffles can be added to the hem to add visual interest to the cape. Measure the ruffle so it is two or three times longer than the hem, then gather it up and stitch it on. Make sure to seal all the seams using a serger, French seaming, flatfelled seams, or seam tape.

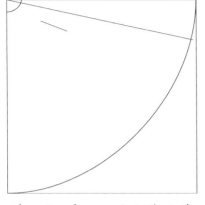

The pattern for a cape is similar to the circular veil.

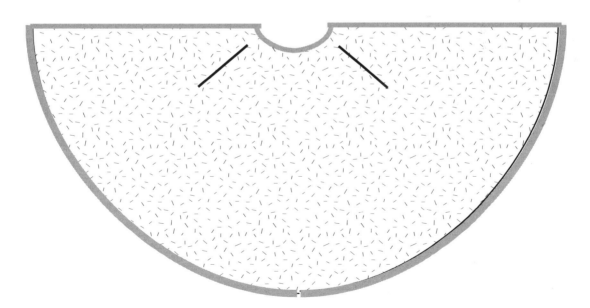

Semi-circular cape with slits for arms.

A dramatic effect can be achieved by stitching a narrow piece of wooden dowel, less than $\frac{1}{4}$" (5 mm) thick into a pocket along the opening seam. This dowel should be cut to hang from fingertip length to the hem. When the dowels are lifted, the cape will extend out to the edge of the dowel like wings, not just from the edge of the fingertips. This can be a very effective and dramatic effect.

Capes can also be made from heavier fabrics to wear as a cover-up between performances or as a wrap for going to and from performances. If it is going to be used only for a cover-up, the decoration can be more dramatic and heavier. The hem in this instance is of less importance and the focus of the decorative elements should be at the chest and neckline areas, drawing attention up to the face.

Historical performers may need a cape or cloak out of necessity for outdoor performances at night or as part of a historic ensemble. Hoods can be added to surround the wearer's head. Hoods can be round or pointed like a Burnoose, with tassels added for a decorative touch. Braid, passementary, ribbon, fur, and contrasting fabric can be used to decorate the outside of the cloak. Make the cloak out of wool, goat, or camel hair when warmth is very important. Line these garments so they fall smoothly over your costume underneath and to increase the warmth. To face the lining, cut it six to ten inches (15–25 cm) narrower than the cloak to accommodate a strip of facing. Close your cloak with a metal clasp, an oriental style frog, or with buttons and loops. For an invisible closure, use large cloak hooks and eyes at the neckline.

Be creative with this garment. Cloaks usually last a long time and you may be wearing it frequently. Include pockets, arm slits, or other features that are useful for your own individual purposes. Be functional and design the garment accordingly.

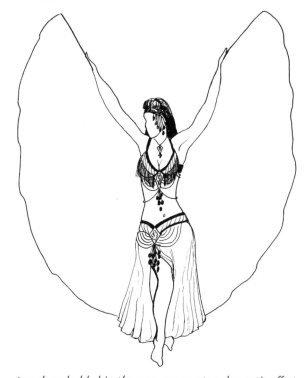

Dowels embedded in the cape can create a dramatic effect.

Artist rendition of an original design by "Julia."

B. CRITES

9 Men's Wear

While it is already difficult to find information about costumes for women, it is nearly impossible to find information about Middle Eastern dancewear for men. There have always been men involved in Middle Eastern dance, although the standard American "Belly Dancer" stereotype has led to much audience surprise when a male dancer takes the stage. Costuming for men walks a fine line. They have to avoid appearing too feminine, which can be a challenge when creating sequined and beaded costumes for a nightclub environment. Many male dancers shy away from floral motifs and soft colors and use sequins and fringe sparingly.

Many of the costume pieces men wear are similar to those worn by ladies. Kaftans, anteri, pants, vests, hats, and turbans are worn by both genders. Men have the added bonus of being able to go without a shirt when they perform. Since the previous chapters have dealt with many of the issues of construction, in this chapter I will focus on the types of looks available for men. All of the construction techniques apply to both men's and women's clothing.

Shirts

Many men wear loose, flowing shirts while performing. These can be rather low cut, laced up the front, or just tied at the neck. The sleeves can be slit to reveal more of the arm and varied cuff styles can dramatically change the look. To make a loose shirt, start out with a standard men's pirate-style shirt pattern. These are available through most standard fabric stores, especially around Halloween. If the shirt is cut short, it can be worn tucked in. If form-fitting pants are worn, the shirt should not make a bulge.

Shirts worn long and cut along historical lines can be worn with more ethnic-styled garments. The standard shirt is composed of rectangles with a gusset under the arm to accommodate movement. The tunic style can be changed by altering the neckline, the shapes of the sleeves and cuffs, and by slitting up the sides. Ribbon and braid can really make the tunic a dynamic style.

There is one other option for men, and that is to go shirtless. If a dancer has a trim enough physique, the dancer can wear a chest harness decorated with fringe and braid. The only suitable chest covering is jewelry, so pile it on. The dancer could also wear arm bands alone to draw attention to his arms without covering the chest.

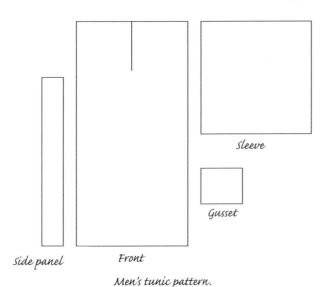

Sleeve

Gusset

Side panel   *Front*

Men's tunic pattern.

shirt with cuffs.

shirt with gathered sleeves.

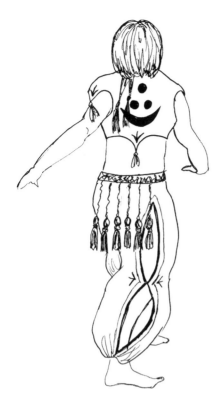

Vests

The vest can be worn with or without a shirt. There are many different shapes to make the vest and it can be very short or reach below the waist. This versatile garment can be very fitted or made loose and boxy. Although it is not exactly equivalent to the women's bra, the vest can be made to match the pants and/or the hip accent to tie the design together. A vest is the perfect showcase for interesting designs either by appliqué, embroidery, or with decorative braid and trim. There are many patterns for vests available on the market today. However, a simple vest can be cut from the measurements of your body out of simple rectangles. Use your widest measurement, either the waist or the chest, add two to four inches (5–10 cm), and then divide in half. This will be the width of the front and back. Draw out three blocks and then change the edges, the neck, and the sleeve to fit the idea in your imagination.

Hip Accent

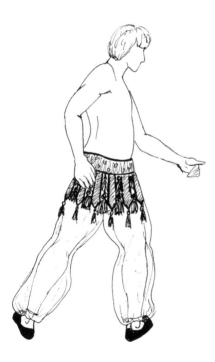

Like the belt worn by women, the hip accent for men is designed to show off and accentuate the subtle movement of the dance. Many male dancers wear scarves that are casually tied and hung from the waist or hips. Some wear cumberbund-like bands made of brocade, satins, or even stretchy sequined fabric. Other performers wear fitted hip bands that have tabs, tassles, and fringe. The method for making a belt is very much the same as for women. Tabs are very popular for hanging from men's belts. Tabs are made by creating strips of fabric, lining them, decorating them, and hanging them from the belt instead of fringe. Tabs can be combined with tassels for even more movement.

Pants

All of the same styles that are worn by women can be utilized by men. A pattern for a pair of sweat pants can be altered to make harem pants. Lowering the hip line and adding fullness and length to the leg will make a simple pair of dance pants. Cuffs at the ankles, choice of fabrics (either sheer or opaque), slits up the sides to show off the legs, or even inset panels of contrasting fabric will play up the pants. Stripes of decorative braid or ribbon can really tie a costume together. If the legs are well shaped, stretch pants in a wide variety of colors can be purchased in dancewear shops. Look at the pants section in the Leg Coverings chapter for more ideas.

Combinations

Like for women, there are garments for men that cover it all. The Turkish anteri can be worn with a full skirt to accent turns. Military stylings and bold, dramatic decorations will add a masculine flair to this unisex garment. The directions for making the man's anteri is the same as for the lady's.

The kaftan can be worn at a variety of different lengths and slit to reveal the pants underneath. Again, the cut is not dramatically different from the layout of the kaftan for women. In Egypt a popular variation, called the *gallibiya*, has a collar and front like a modern Western-style shirt, but from the waist down is a flowing garment.

Head coverings

There are four major head covering styles. One is to wrap a cotton square over the head for a Gypsy look. Wearing the *kaffiyeh,* or head cloth, with an *agal* (decorative bands of cord). This style is worn with ethnic-looking garments and can lend a note of mystery to the costume. A turban is especially effective when worn with historic and folkloric costumes. The manner for tying a turban is described in the Accessories chapter. The last type of head dress that is common in men's dance wear is the hat: flat hat, pill box hat, or fez. This style can be worn with many different styles of dress depending on the choice of fabrics and the style of decoration.

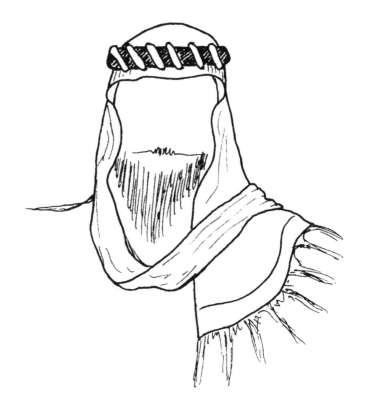

Bedouin man wearing a hirz.

10 Accessories

Accessories

Many different accessories can be made to match your costume to enhance the total look. Dancers will frequently make chokers, bracelets, fitted sleeves, anklets, and head pieces to accent or blend into their finished ensemble. These can be made easily with the scraps of fabric left over from constructing the larger costume pieces or from contrasting materials. Jewelry can also be used to finish an ensemble. Use your imagination when coming up with ideas—you never know when you could start a new fashion with an unusual trademark accent. Use accessories to draw attention to your best features. If you have a long, elegant neck, make a fitted choker. If you want to cover marks or scars on your arms, make cuffs or bracelets. If you feel your feet are your best feature, use anklets or foot covers to make them really stand out.

Matching Accessories

Accessories are worn by most dancers to accentuate the movements of their arms. These can be as narrow as a bracelet, extended to the elbow as a gauntlet, or all the way to the top of the arm for a long, fitted sleeve. Sleeve puffs can also cover the biceps. Often these accessories are made to exactly match the costume so similar bead work, appliqués, and trim are often used to tie the look together. Other dancers invest in an ensemble of accessories in a neutral color scheme such as silver, gold, black, or red. If most of your costumes have gold accents, make your accessories in gold and they will be useful for more than one costume.

Most arm decorations that are worn below the elbow are made stiff and firm by building them with a lining of heavy interfacing. The first three arm decorations to the left, the bracelet, the cuff, and the gauntlet are all made using the same directions below:

1. Measure your arm at the points where the bottom edge and the top edge of the garment will lie across the arm. Transfer these marking to paper, making them the distance apart that you have decided upon and make sure that these lines are parallel.

2. Add a half an inch (1 cm) to the sides to accommodate the closure. The interfacing will be cut directly from this pattern. Cut the lining fabric and your covering fabric half an inch bigger all the way around to accommodate a seam allowance.

3. Stitch the covering fabric on first, folding the edges under all the way around the interfacing. You can sew it either by machine or by hand. Take the lining fabric and fold it half an inch under and press well. Hand stitch or machine stitch the lining to the bottom, covering all raw edges.

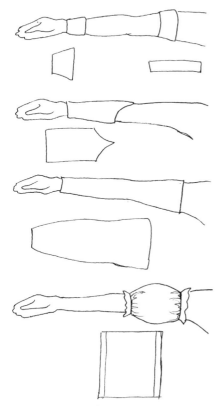

Greek necklace.

Patterns for arm coverings.

4. Trim as desired.

5. Hand stitch a row of Velcro along the closure. Make sure the hook side is pointed away from your skin. The loop (fuzzy) side will not scratch your skin.

You can use the above directions for making collars as well, only measure your neck instead. Some dancers do not like using Velcro at the neckline as it can get tangled in the hair. Large flat hooks and eyes will provide a secure closure if you have a similar distaste. Hooks can also be used for cuffs and gauntlets, but they can be difficult to hook with one hand.

Sleeve puffs are simply rectangles of fabric with casings for elastic. These can be made to any desired fullness and length. For very sheer fabrics, you may want to add a row of bias or twill tape to add strength and create the casing. Run the elastic through and try it on, adjusting the elastic for a perfect fit.

For a long fitted sleeve, use a fabric that contains lycra or elastic to achieve a smooth fit. Again, you will need to measure the arm at several points and transfer these measurements to paper. Add seam allowance to the pattern and use it to create your sleeves. If the fabric you choose is not as stretchy, you may want to put a casing at the top and run a piece of elastic through just to give the sleeve that extra help to stay up.

A foot cover is an anklet with a triangular or rectangular piece that extends towards the toes. A loop is attached at the end to wrap around the middle or big toes as an anchor to keep it from moving while dancing. Experiment with different shapes using paper until you achieve the look you want. Use the paper as a guide for cutting out the final accessory. Add a layer of interfacing to stiffen the piece, cover it, and line as in the directions above.

Be creative with these little pieces. If you don't sew, you can purchase items from different vendors. But if you know how to crochet, try making a pair using that technique. If you quilt, how about little pieced garments out of glitzy fabrics? Use your imagination and come up with garments that are as distinctive as you are.

Head bands can top off the costume by framing your face and carrying the design elements all the way up. Head bands come in a wide variety of shapes and sizes. Play with hair ornaments in stores to see what the possibilities are. Clusters of barrettes, pill box hats, and headbands can draw attention to your face and hair. Necklaces can be adjusted to fit across the forehead or elasticized trim can be turned into a simple band. If you are really creative, you can make a fitted headband with interfacing using the directions for the cuffs and collars above and bead it to match your bra and belt. Beaded or chainette fringe can be hung across the forehead and down the sides of your face to frame it. You are limited only by your imagination.

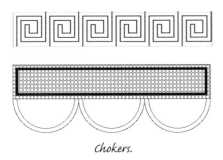

Chokers.

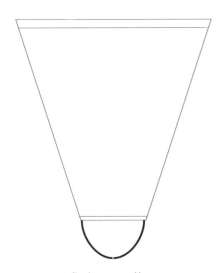

Foot cover pattern.

Above: cabaret dancer with foot cover, choker, and bracelets made to match costume.

Jewelry

There is a wide variety of jewelry styles that can be worn with Middle Eastern dance wear. Jewelry should be chosen to harmonize with the look and style of the costume. Because there are so many different styles, looks, and materials to choose from, this section will focus on the areas wear jewelry can be incorporated into the overall design and on the distinctive Middle Eastern style jewelry.

Jewelry can be worn in a variety of different locations. The two illustrations on the left show the possible options for choice in jewelry. Starting from the top down these are the locations where jewelry can be incorporated into your design:

- On the head, anklets can cover the forehead. Necklaces can be woven into turbans. Pill box hats or a fez can be covered with a draped anklet or necklace or covered with decorative pins.

- Earrings of all varieties can be worn. Things that dangle will accentuate your movements, hoops will give that gypsy look. There are also imported ethnic styles with bells, coins, or other medallions.

- Necklaces come in so many styles that attempting to list them all would be fruitless. However, things to look for are styles that go with your outfit and do not interfere with your veil wraps.

- Stomach drapes can be made of jewelry pieces of all sorts. They can be suspended by safety pins from the lower edge of the bra. Earrings can become focal pieces on the bra straps or on the cups. Collars and anklets, when you have a matched set, can be draped over the cups and stitched down as a decorative element.

- A long chain or strand of pearls can be worn around the torso at the stomach to draw attention to this area. Some dancers even learn to maneuver their belly chain during their dance.

- Chains and jewelry pieces can be incorporated into the design of the belt. Pins make great focal pieces and necklaces can drape down like fringe. Entire bra and belt ensembles can be decorated just with jewelry.

- On the arms, bracelets worn on the biceps, forearm, or wrist can be a nice accent. Having multiple bracelets allows dancers to mix and match—or even to wear them all—depending on the look they are trying to achieve. Rings on the fingers can also be a nice finishing touch, although they may interfere with zill work, so test them before going into performance.

- The ankles and feet can be a great site for application of jewelry. Try wearing bracelets as anklets or making a matched set of cuffs. Foot covers that link to anklets and wrap round the toe can be found ready-made, or constructed out of jewelry bits. And don't forget toe rings; if you are going barefoot or wearing sandals, you can accentuate your feet.

Be creative and unafraid to pile it on. The added motion emphasis as well as the soft clinking of large jewelry pieces will help to create the mood of the dance. Shop around and exchange jewelry pieces with friends for new looks. A large collection of jewelry will allow you to create new looks with familiar costumes. Look for pieces that fit the theme of your costume. Coins, snakes, beads, chains, and pearls are can all be incorporated into costume jewelry. Keep your eyes open whenever you're out shopping.

Bedouin, Ethnic, and Tribal Jewelry

People in the Middle East, both men and women, wear large quantities of jewelry and metal ornamentation. The styles vary from region to region but there are some standard pieces that are worn frequently and are available at import stores and through vendors who cater to the dance community. Below is a brief list of the types of pieces that are available. Keep in mind that every style can be found in a range of materials from brass to silver, from nickel to gold. Buy pieces that you can afford, and when you get them, clean them carefully. Often, pieces made of less expensive materials have gems and stones that are held in by wax rather than glue, so be prepared. If you find a great piece that is missing some stones, head off to your local bead shop and search. You may be able to replace missing gems for a small investment of time and money.

Simply put, ethnic jewelry from the Middle East has some design features that you will want to look for. They may have lots of heavy, large metal pieces with applied surface designs that follow the form of the outer edge of the main elements or lots of dangling chains with bells, balls, or small shaped medallions hanging from them, often at different lengths. Jewelry is worn on the head covering, across the forehead, at the sides of the face, at the neck, and across the chest area. Cuffs and bracelets are popular, as are belts. Men frequently wear knives with elaborately worked metal sheaths.

Motifs in this type of jewelry usually have amuletic properties to keep away the evil eye. Crescent moons, stars, flowers, and geometric patterns are common motifs that are worked in metal. The Hand of Fatimah (see page 114) is one of the most frequently worn amuletic motifs worn to guard against evil. Below are some of the main types of jewelry worn.

Hirz: This is an amulet case, worn as a pendant from the neck. They can come in a variety of different shapes including squares, rectangles, hollow tubes, and crescents. Often, they have dangles hanging from them. These cases usually contain a prayer or quote from the Koran and can be found throughout many Islamic countries. Sometimes they are suspended on chains, but they can also be found on black cord or strung with beads.

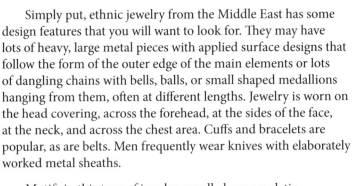

Three hirz, worn on chains or cords..

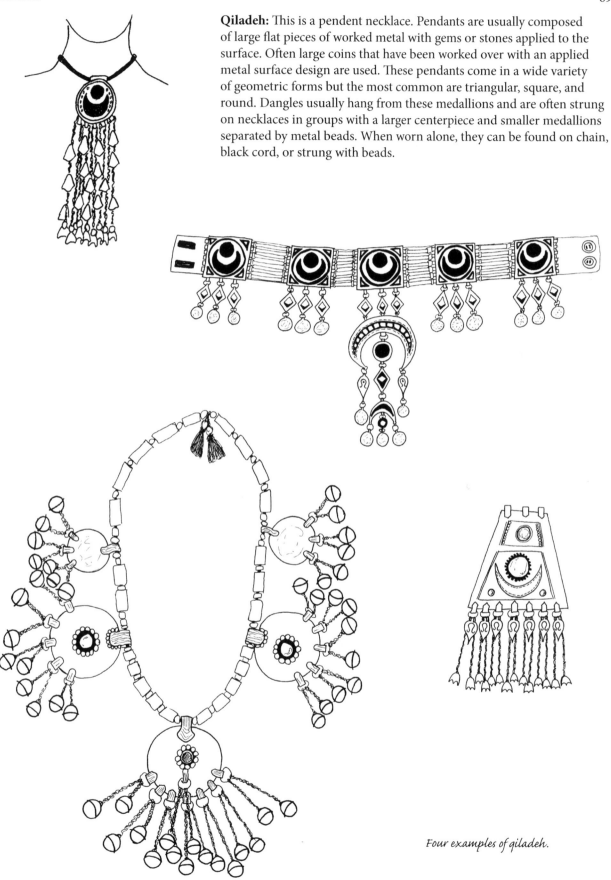

Qiladeh: This is a pendent necklace. Pendants are usually composed of large flat pieces of worked metal with gems or stones applied to the surface. Often large coins that have been worked over with an applied metal surface design are used. These pendants come in a wide variety of geometric forms but the most common are triangular, square, and round. Dangles usually hang from these medallions and are often strung on necklaces in groups with a larger centerpiece and smaller medallions separated by metal beads. When worn alone, they can be found on chain, black cord, or strung with beads.

Four examples of qiladeh.

Khatim.

Shaf: A nose ornament. In some tribes, the nose is pierced and ornaments are inserted. These can vary is size from a small bead to a large and dramatic ring with inset gems and dangling beads.

Khatim: Ring. Rings can be found everywhere, usually made of silver or out of a silver-colored metal. Often rings are inset with stones or decorated with a metal design. Rings are typically heavier, thicker, and more substantial than their western counterparts.

Bangar: Bracelet. These can vary from narrow bands that slip over the wrist to elaborate hinged cuffs with decorative metalwork and inset beads. Like most tribal style jewelry, these pieces can vary dramatically from region to region, so get what you like.

This is only a small sample of the types of jewelry available. Look for pieces that contain real stones rather than glass gems. Stones that are used a great deal include: carnelian, garnet, agates, turquoise, amber, coral, and lapis. Beads can also be made of *faience* (ceramic) or glass in the popular colors of red, blue, and green.

Four examples of bangar.

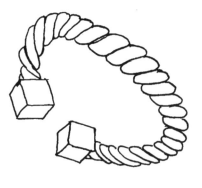

Hats and Headdresses

Dancers have many options for head wear. From elaborate barrettes and decorative hats to headscarves and turbans, there is a wide selection of different styles available. Head wear should harmonize with your costume stylistically. If you are making a beaded ensemble, perhaps a decorative headband or beaded pill box style hat would accent it perfectly. A full tiered skirt with blouse and vest might best be topped with a gypsy-styled, fringed head cloth. A historically-inspired yelek would go best with a turban.

Below is a quick list of different head covering styles.

Decorative hair jewelry can be barrettes with trim that matches your ensemble, made of plain metal, or beaded with gems or pearls. Small appliqués can be hot glued directly onto metal hair clips. Store-bought headbands can be painted with fabric glue, trimmed with ribbons or braid, or even beaded to match. Look for ready-made items, especially at Christmas and New Year's when silver and gold accessories are in all the stores.

Pill box hats can top off either a historic or a cabaret-styled costume depending on the materials from which it is constructed. Patterns and instructions for construction of little hats are available from all major pattern companies. Hats can also be purchased ready-made through Middle Eastern dancewear vendors and at import stores. Keep your eyes peeled for hats with elaborate embroidery and rich, sumptuous fabrics. Old pill box hats can be recycled with the addition of chains and coins as long as the hat is stiff and firm enough to hold the weight. Experiment with decorative trims until you have created something distinctive, yet versatile. Especially when making historical, or folkloric costumes, pieces don't have to match, but rather, harmonize in contrasting fabric or colors.

For gypsy styles and with cotton beladi dresses, a simple head scarf can do the trick. With a cabaret costume, a beaded scarf can be found to match any basic colored outfit. A black and silver or black and gold beaded scarf can be a very dramatic addition. For a more ethnic look, make or buy a scarf edged with coins, fringe, and decorative braid and trim. A piece of jewelry can be stitched along the edge of a head scarf and draped across the forehead. Beaded fringe can also be attached to a headband along with a scarf to create a very pharonic-styled headdress.

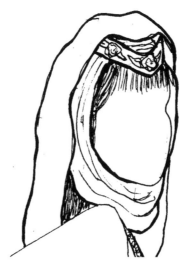

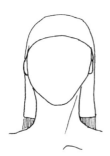

Turbans are very effective with historical, folkloric, and tribal-styled outfits. There are many ways to tie a turban. Turbans vary greatly in length and width. The fabric can be anywhere from four to twelve inches (10–30 cm) wide and three to ten yards (meters) long. One effective method for wrapping a turban is:

1. Center the turban over your head so the ends hang down the sides over the ears. Twist the fabric to form a loose cord.

2. Pull both ends to the back of the head. Twist one side over the other and then bring to the front. This means that the right side will go to the back, twist around the left, and then go back to the right.

3. Bring ends to the front and pass them one at a time over the front of the head. They now have switched sides, but have not twisted.

4. Repeat steps 2 and 3 until you have about a foot of fabric left. At this point you can tuck your fabric in to secure your turban, or you can leave one edge hanging behind, or even bring one edge under your chin and tuck on the other side.

For an alternate look, twist the turban at the front of the head, and let it pass over and under in the back. If you want to tie in two colors, do one color at a time, doing steps 2 and 3 in one color and then 2 and 3 again in the second until the head is covered. If you are using scarves with tassels on the end, you may want to line the fabric up until you have the ends finishing at the sides of the head.

Turbans are more comfortable when made out of natural fibers such as cotton, linen, silk, or ramie. If your hair is slippery, you may want to wear the turban over a headcloth. A small turban can also be tied over a tarboosh or a fez. A veil worn over the turban will frame the face and provide another layer of visual interest to the costume.

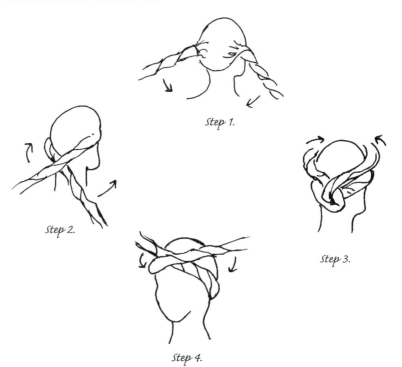

Step 1.

Step 2.

Step 3.

Step 4.

Berber style turban.

11 Details

Color

When you are designing your costume, usually the first thing that comes to mind is the color. The selection of colors for the finished costume is a very personal experience that reflects the emotional state of the dancer. Virtually any color can be used to create a belly dance costume. In the Middle and Far East, bright and richly saturated colors are used with great abandon to break the monotony of the outside desert world. Only outside the home will you see black-cloaked women scurrying about. Once safely ensconced in the privacy of her home, an Arabian woman will wear beautiful clothing full of color, pattern, and movement.

Many colors have emotional significance. White is used in the Middle East as a mourning color, very much the way black is worn in our society. Red is a color that symbolizes passion and blood and is worn by brides in many areas of the Near and Far east. By the same token, blue is the color of the sky, the sea, power, and peace. Green represents the land, but it is also a holy color that is worn by devout people who have made the pilgrimage to Mecca. Many women, especially in war torn countries, wear the colors of their flags as a show of solidarity.

Once you have decided to create your own costume, think about the colors that make you feel good, happy, and joyous. If there is a color you really like, you can turn it into a costume with style and grace. If you have had your colors analyzed you know which ones will look good on you. I strongly recommend that you consider what you like instead of what someone suggests you should like. If you are pale, you may want to play up the translucence of your skin with rich gem-like colors which would make a color analyst cringe. Remember that this is a costume; you will be wearing a good deal of makeup and you will be moving around. Contrasts between the colors of the costume and your flesh tones will only emphasize the movement of your body and force the viewer's eye to move around your entire figure and costume.

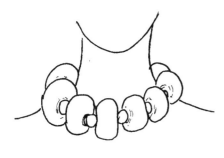

Top: amber necklace.
Above: Greek earrings.
Below: Greek bracelet.

If you are making your bra and belt so that you can combine different skirts with them, you will want to choose the colors to get the greatest amount of use. Metallics come into play here. Many experienced dancers recommend that novice performers start with a basic metallic belt of either gold or silver. Metallics are the belly dancer's neutral color. A silver bra and belt can go with almost every color skirt you can imagine. If you want the ultimate in versatility, use a combination of silver, gold, and copper. With this belt, you could not only wear it with a wide variety of skirts, but you will not have to color-coordinate trims, either. All the colors will be right there, already matching. Be aware of the variations available in gold and silver tones. There are pale bronze golden shades, deep rich gold, white silver, or antiqued variations with touches of black; some of these shades do not combine or blend well so be selective and choose your metallic tones with care. Two other colors that are staples in Middle Eastern dance wardrobes are black and red. However, if you feel an affinity to blue and want to incorporate a shade of blue into every costume, then perhaps making a blue bra and belt will be best to start with.

If you are more interested in a total color effect, you will want your belt's color or hue to match the skirts, veil, and bra. In this case you must choose a color scheme that you are truly happy with. You will be seen head to toe in this single color, so make sure you *really* like it. If you are going for a monochromatic costume, you may want to consider different intensities of the same color to create a more visually stimulating costume.

There are times when you will have some fabric or are thinking of buying a used costume where the color might not be exactly what you want. In these cases, look beyond just the color. Try it on and see what happens when you move. If the costume fits you and you are happy with everything but the color, consider this point: most dance clubs or restaurants have lighting that will alter colors, sometimes in unusual ways. Blue under yellow light will look green, for instance. The color you try on may not be the actual color you wear at the time of your performance. Light can also be detrimental to the color; for example, there are shades of purple that can turn muddy brown under green lights.

Middle Eastern Motifs

A motif is a design element that is used repeatedly throughout an entire costume or in one key focal place. The use of a motif will give the costume a finished and complete look. Even if you choose to combine a wide range of colors or materials, a repeated design element will form a visual link between the costume elements.

Turkish floral motifs.

Greek meander.

Design from Turkish plate featuring ogival patterns.

There are an infinite number of designs available. Everything you see can be turned into a design element. Throughout the centuries in the Middle East, floral imagery has been used to decorate everything from clothing to books to buildings. What is known today as an *arabesque*, or swirling line, is one of these traditional floral motifs. Paisley also comes from the Middle East and uses smooth flowing lines to border the edges of the form. Scroll work and knot designs were also prevalent as well.

Some dancers choose a specific locale and take frequently-used symbols to decorate their costumes. The Greek meander, or key pattern, is used frequently by dancers on ribbons and trims. Other typical Greek motifs are grapes, vases, flowing white robes, geometric animals and florals, acanthus leaves, and spirals.

Turkish-inspired patterns include ogival patterns, çintemani (three dot patterns), as well as crescent moons and large floral patterns. Red, gold, and green have been favorites of the Turks since the days of Sulyman. Study Turkish textiles, pottery, and metal work for interesting patterns and designs to copy. Each area developed its own unique styles so look for Persian motifs, such as the *boteh* (better known as the paisley), or for Mogul designs.

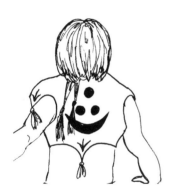

Çintemani pattern on vest.

Turkish teapot.

Turkish floral motif.

Turkish anteri.

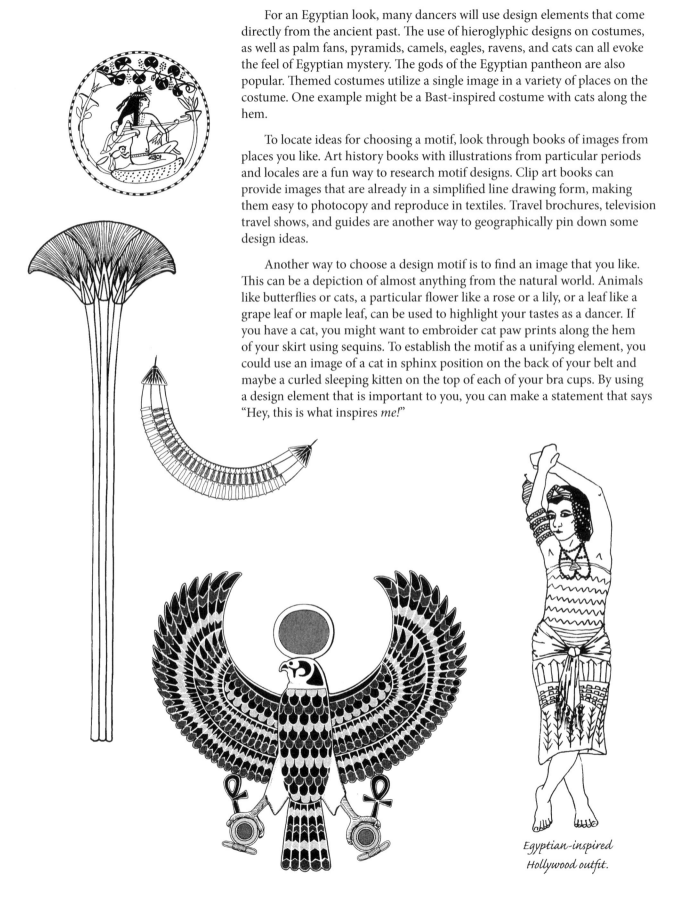

For an Egyptian look, many dancers will use design elements that come directly from the ancient past. The use of hieroglyphic designs on costumes, as well as palm fans, pyramids, camels, eagles, ravens, and cats can all evoke the feel of Egyptian mystery. The gods of the Egyptian pantheon are also popular. Themed costumes utilize a single image in a variety of places on the costume. One example might be a Bast-inspired costume with cats along the hem.

To locate ideas for choosing a motif, look through books of images from places you like. Art history books with illustrations from particular periods and locales are a fun way to research motif designs. Clip art books can provide images that are already in a simplified line drawing form, making them easy to photocopy and reproduce in textiles. Travel brochures, television travel shows, and guides are another way to geographically pin down some design ideas.

Another way to choose a design motif is to find an image that you like. This can be a depiction of almost anything from the natural world. Animals like butterflies or cats, a particular flower like a rose or a lily, or a leaf like a grape leaf or maple leaf, can be used to highlight your tastes as a dancer. If you have a cat, you might want to embroider cat paw prints along the hem of your skirt using sequins. To establish the motif as a unifying element, you could use an image of a cat in sphinx position on the back of your belt and maybe a curled sleeping kitten on the top of each of your bra cups. By using a design element that is important to you, you can make a statement that says "Hey, this is what inspires *me!*"

Egyptian-inspired Hollywood outfit.

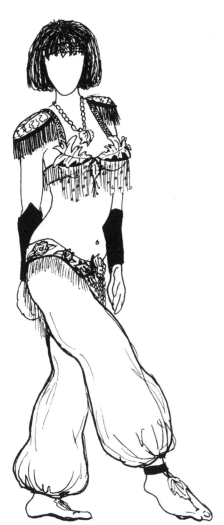

As long as you choose something you like and use the design in more than one location, your motif will become the visual glue that pulls your costume together and makes it work.

Hints for choosing a motif:

1. Keep the line drawing simple. The fewer the lines the easier it will be to translate the design.

2. Pick an image that can be made larger or smaller so that you can stretch and manipulate it to fit into different portions of your costume.

3. Choose an image that is not offensive. Stay away from images that might be considered offensive due to their ethnic, religious, or sexual content.

4. Be creative and keep your eyes open. You never know when you might spot the perfect image.

Using a Motif

Once you have chosen a single motif or a combination of motifs, use them in the design of your costume. Make appliqués or do beadwork directly onto the costume in the shape of the chosen designs. Explore your options of where to place the motifs. The main motif should always appear on the bra and belt. If you are making matching cuffs, head band, collar, and anklets, place smaller versions of the motif in those places as well. Tie your costume together through the use of a motif and you will look totally pulled together.

Floral appliqués are usually the easiest to find pre-made. When you purchase your appliqués, make sure to get enough for the entire project. Choose the location, say, one on each bra cup, two on the back and one on the front of the belt. Depending upon the size, you may need more or less, so buy in accordance to what you will use. If you find one fabulous applique, buy it. You can always hand make smaller versions, or purchase similar items to tie a look together.

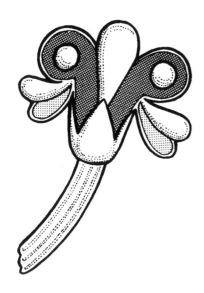

Fabrics and Trims

There are an infinite variety of materials with which you can create Middle Eastern dancewear. From sumptuous silks and brocades to linen and guaze, your choices are limited only by the time and money you are planning on spending on your costume.

Fabrics

There are many different fabrics available on the retail market that can be used to create belly dance costumes. There are numerous brand names and subtle variations in fiber content and surface finish. Below is a brief list of the types of fabric used by many dancers.

Chiffon: A light to medium weight softly woven fabric that is used to create the filmy full skirts and veils that are traditionally associated with the dance. It comes in a variety of weights from the ultra sheer to opaque. Chiffon is also available in prints.

Lamé: This is a stiff woven metallic fabric that has a great deal of body and shine. It doesn't drape well, but it can be used to create skirts and veils and to cover belts and bras. It comes in a variety of formats with variations in the weight. Also comes in prints.

Acrylic foil: These are relatively new on the market. These fabrics are often knitted with a metallic layer bonded to the outer surface. These fabrics are easy to handle because they do not fray. They drape well and produce a great deal of shine. There are variations where the foil is applied in small circles or in swirls.

Dress silkies: Many fabrics are lumped together under this rather strange-sounding title. These textiles are woven polyester fibers that produce a shiny, smooth, drapable fabric in a variety of weights and textures. These are often printed and make excellent skirts and veils. This type of fabric also makes a good cover for bras and belts.

Satin: This fabric comes in a variety of fiber contents and is identified by the unique weave. They come in two standard types: woven satin or crepe-backed satin. Woven satin is rather stiff and makes a good bra and belt cover. Crepe-backed satin is soft, drapes well, and is good for skirts and belts.

Brocade: These are heavy fabrics often found in the upholstery section of fabric stores. Woven in multiple colors and in multiple layers, these patterned fabrics make an excellent cover for bras and belts.

Flat lace: Many flat laces are available with metallic embroidered designs. Lace can be used for a variety of purposes but often is very sheer and needs to be lined. Be aware that due to the openness of the weave or knit of lace it can be prone to snagging on beads and hair.

This is by no means a complete list of available fabric types and should be used as a guide. Many new types of weaves and knits are always appearing in the fabric stores. Check the shops in your area to find out what is available near you. Fabric prices can vary widely depending on your location and the particular store. Plan a budget before you go out shopping to prevent a major pinch in the ol' pocket book.

If you find a piece of dynamite fabric, but you can only afford a single yard, your can use it in pieces in interesting ways. Here is a list of items you could make with a single yard of fabric.

1. Two decorative panels to wear over a fuller skirt or, if you are slender, to form a fitted skirt. If a yard isn't long enough, add a ruffle of a contrasting or blending chiffon or organza to make it the correct length.

2. Make an ensemble of accessories. Make a headband, cuffs, collar, and matching anklets to really pull together a finished look. Use less expensive fabrics for the lining.

3. Cover a bra and belt. A really exciting fabric can make a bra and belt that needs little embellishment. Just add a few appliqués, coins, and fringe and your costume is finished.

4. Make a vest and trim a pair of pants with the fabric at the cuffs. This is really good way to stretch a small bit of fabric and yet tie an outfit together.

5. Create a hip wrap and scarf set. Cut the fabric into two triangles, a big one for the hips and a small one for the head. Use the leftover fabric to extend the ties on the hip wrap. You can wear a metal belt, tassel belt, or even a cabaret-styled belt over this hip treatment.

Braids.

Braid and Fringe

Many designers use gold or fabric braid on their costumes. There is a great deal of variety in both the materials and designs of braid. Search for braid not only in regular fabric stores, but in upholstery stores and in craft shops. The after-Christmas sales can be a boon for designers looking for gold braid and other decorative trims. Use them as individual items, or layer them by placing them one next to the other to create larger bands of decoration. This can be applied on the tops of bra cups and along the upper or lower edges of your belt. Don't forget that lightweight braid can be used to decorate the hems of skirts, kaftans, and pants.

Textile fringe can be purchased in most fabric and upholstery stores. This fringe is called chainette, which refers to the manner in which the individual threads are made. This fringe comes in standard colors such as gold, black, red, blue, and purple, but sometimes it can be found in the current hot decorating colors. Fringe comes in several lengths and can be layered. For instance, you can layer 12" black fringe with 6" gold fringe and another row of 2" black on top. Decorative braid can be placed over the top edge of the fringe if it is unsightly. Another way to punch up chainette is to stitch paitlettes onto individual strands. They can be lined up or sprinkled about in matching or contrasting colors.

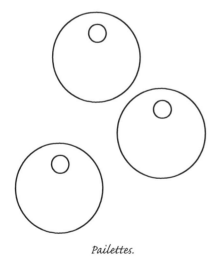

Pailettes.

Dangling Coins

The tradition of decorating the dancing costume with coins dates back to the origins of the dance itself. At one time, the dance was used as worship. Devout worshippers would pay the church for the performances. Money was tossed at the dancer's feet. Later, Gypsy performers would perform in public venues. Patrons would toss money at their feet as well. However, not having the shelter of a temple to protect them, these Gypsy women needed another method of protecting their wealth. By putting it in plain sight, but in inaccessible locations, they achieved a form of open, yet protected display of their wealth. They sewed the coins directly onto their clothing or spent their money on flashy jewelry. This tradition of using coins to decorate costumes has been brought down to us today and is a part of most historically inspired costumes. In some parts of the Third World, this method of wearing one's wealth is common, especially among Bedouin tribes whose existence depends on mobility. Jewelry is one method of compressing wealth into a very tiny object.

Coin belt with tassels.

There are several ways to attach coins to a costume:

1. Sew the coin on with sturdy carpet thread, dental floss, beading thread, or even braided fishing wire. Be sure to make large loops so that the coins will hang free. After making several loops, tie off the coin. Then go back and bundle the loops together. This will encourage your coins to move more, but they may spin if they are small.

2. Attach a jump ring or other metal extender to the coin and sew that onto the garment. This will allow for movement, but if the jump ring is not sealed, then the coin may work itself free.

3. Attach the coin to chain with a jump ring, and then stitch the chain onto the garment. This will have even more movement than the previous two formats. Again, you will want to make sure that the jump rings are firmly closed, or even soldered shut, to avoid both loosing coins or catching open loops on other costume pieces, such as veils.

4. Lightweight coins can be strung onto a length of thin crochet thread and then crocheted into a pattern. This has a distinctive lacy effect. Many of the vendors listed in the back of the book sell scarves and veils with this type of decoration.

When adding your coins think about your pattern. If filling in a large area, such as a bra cup, start from the bottom and work your way to the top. Each row of coins should slightly touch and overlap the previous row. If you want the bottom row of coins to lay flat along the cup, you can glue them down to the surface with fabric glue.

Coins can also be very effective when combined with chainette or fabric fringe. You can sprinkle small lightweight coins throughout the fringe, stitching the loops to individual strands of the chainette. Alternatively, coins can be placed in a row between two rows of chainette so they poke through, or even in a row along the top edge to conceal the thick top stitching of the chainette. Varieties abound!

Beads

We could write a whole book about beads. There are an infinite variety of beads available through retail and wholesale sources. Beads can be made of glass, crystal, plastic, or ceramic. Beads are used to make appliqués for surface designs as well as to create the beaded fringe that hang off the costume and emphasizes the movement of the performer. They come pre-formed on strands or loose in small or large quantities and in a tremendous amount of colors and shapes. Among the countless variety of shapes are

Pearls: These beads imitate the look of naturally created pearls and will have a soft, rich luster. They come in several main shapes including drops, rounds, and oblongs. The luster will often vary in color from white to pink to black.

Bugles: These long narrow beads have a tubular shape. They can be as small as 2 mm up to ultra long 40 mm. Bugles come with smooth or faceted surfaces and in a wide variety of colors.

Faceted beads: These beads come in different flat cuts that are molded into the surface of the beads. Faceted beads are reflective on the flat surfaces and create shimmering effects on a moving costume. They, too, come in a untold varieties of sizes, shapes, and colors.

The method of attaching beads to a costume *is* a book unto itself. I recommend checking the bibliography for good sources on applying beads. The quickest way to gain the most valuable information would be to take a class or workshop on beading. The only special supplies that are needed are: beads, beading needles, beading thread (although some seamstress swear by dental floss), beeswax, a thimble, and something to cut the thread. Often beading goes smoother when the fabric is pulled taught, so you may want to place your beading work into an embroidery hoop. Below are some very simplified beading techniques.

Stitching directly onto fabric: The thread is knotted from the wrong side. The thread is pulled up to the right side. The bead is threaded onto the needle and is stitched down. To avoid spilling large quantities of beads, knot your thread every few beads. That way if one goes, they don't all go. Fill in areas of your design.

Creating beaded fringe: Fringe is usually made on a separate piece of tape or ribbon and then is applied to the garment. Cut the tape to the proper size and baste it to a larger piece of fabric. Place this fabric and tape in an embroidery hoop. Knot the thread on the wrong side of tape. String on a row of beads. At the bottom, you can tie it off and clip the thread. (Make sure to reinforce this knot with a dab of glue!) Alternatively, you can place a small bead at the end and then rethread back up through all of the beads, going over the last smaller bead. When you get back to the tape, knot the thread and begin the process again.

Large gems with dual holes: These beads can be easily sewn onto fabric in a manner similar to sewing on a button. Knot the thread and pull up through the fabric then down through the hole. Repeat until sturdy, then pull the thread to the wrong side and knot.

A combination of beaded fringe and swags.

Beading is very time-consuming and many dancers prefer using appliqués with beads on them and buying pre-made beaded fringe. Many belly dance suppliers carry beaded fringe imported from the Middle East. This fringe is generally made of small seed beads and has very densely packed strands of beads. If you buy pre-made beads, take the precautionary step of placing a drop of glue at the bottom of each strand. An ounce of prevention can help your costume last.

Sequins

Sequins are rounded flat or cupped pieces of laminated acrylic that shine brightly in light. These little doodads come in different sizes, shapes, and colors. They are often used in conjunction with beads to create appliquéed surfaces. Pailettes are large round flat sequins with the hole placed closer to one side. These can be combined with beads to create fringe. Sequins also come cut into a variety of unusual shapes such as leaves, stars, geometric shapes, and even snowflakes.

Sequins are applied in much the same manner as beads, and often in conjunction with beads. Standard sequins come in two formats: individually or loose in long strings. Loose sequins take more time and often have to be sewn on by hand. Strands of sequins can be sewn on by machine if you use a sharp needle and sew in the direction of the sequins so they lie flat rather than bunching up under the foot.

Strings of sequins can be used to create large expanses of sequined areas by covering the fabric with the sequins and then stitching them on by machine. Multiple strands of different colors can be used to create patterns and add texture quickly and inexpensively. If you are putting sequins on in rows, stitch towards the edge of the sequin that will be layered under the next row, like putting shingles on a roof. This will cover the machine stitching. Iron-on sequins are also available. You can make your own iron-ons using fusable webbing. Test this process first on a scrap to make sure that both the sequins and the base fabric can handle the necessary heat.

Fabric glue can be used to attach sequins, jewels, and beads. Acrylic fabric paint can also be used to attach beads and sequins as it has glue-like properties and can accentuate your design with its color.

If you are worried about committing to a long, intensive beading project, start with creating your own appliqués. Use clip art books to find a design that will work for you. Some books even have iron transfer patterns that you can place right onto your fabric. Try different techniques—hand sewing, machine sewing, fusing, and gluing—to see what methods work for you. You may like it so much that you go on to create garment after garment.

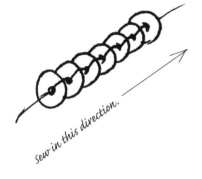

Sew in this direction.

Shisha

Popular in fusion garments , this Indian technique is used to attach mirrors to the surface of fabrics using embroidery to hold the edges down. This technique was very popular during the 17th century and examples have been found all over the Middle East. Mirrors can be found in many different sizes and shapes. Hand blown mirrors are often found in irregular shapes, the shape of the embroidery giving them the appearance of being perfectly round.

There are many different techniques for making shisha. Below are directions for one type of shisha. There are several books on this style of embroidery available. Check other sources for ideas for incorporating this technique into larger designs or for alternative stitches.

Step 1.

1. The first step is to create a base of threads across the surface of the mirror. Figure A and B show two different types of bases.

Step 2.

2. The filler stitch is worked around the mirror. If the tension is loose, more of the thread will show. If the tension is tight, more of the mirror will show. These stitches can be formed using a number of different stitches. Figure C shows a simple shisha stitch. Other stitches such as the buttonhole stitch and the herringbone stitch can be used.

3. Continue around the entire mirror, making sure to maintain a uniform thread tension so the circle is as round and centered as possible. Finish off by knotting the thread on the back of the piece. Glue threads to ensure a longer life and reinforce the work.

Alternatively, large mirrors can be applied using a reverse appliqué technique. This involves several steps:

Step 3.

1. Mark the mirror placement on the back of the top layer of fabric. Trace the mirror using a chalk pencil or disappearing ink pen.

2. Draw the same shape 1/4" (5 mm) inside the traced line.

3. Cut on the line.

4. Press the fabric 1/8" back and stitch down.

5. Center the mirror under the opening and above the backing fabric. You may want to hold the mirror down with a dab of fabric glue for added strength and to keep it from shifting.

6. Stitch around the outside edge of the mirror. This can be done by machine using a zipper foot, or it can be done by hand with bright contrasting thread. Ornamental stitches add to the finished product.

Embroidery is very popular throughout the Middle East and each region has its own particular design vocabulary and feel to the finished product. In Palestine, geometric embroidery in combinations of black and red are popular, while in Turkey, colorful embroidery in floral motifs are more common. There are many design sources for embroidery; check your local library or bookstore to see what is available in your area.

Sixteenth-century Turkish designs suitable for embroidery or appliqué.

12 Going Professional

Perhaps you have made several costumes for yourself and a friend has asked you to help her out with a costume. Maybe you have been sewing professionally for many years and are ready to dip into the Middle Eastern dance arena. No matter where you fall between these two extremes, making costumes for others can be challenging, rewarding, and lucrative. Although the topic of owning and running a costuming business could fill an entire book alone, this chapter will briefly go over some of the issues related specifically to the world of Middle Eastern dancewear.

Before I begin, let me first say that there are several good books on the market that deal with the issue of running a sewing business. The three books that have most influenced my own business are:

Sew to Success, by Kathleen Spike
The "Business" of Sewing, by Barbara Wright Sykes
Homemade Money, by Barbara Brabec

These books give information on setting up and running a tailoring, custom sewing, or craft business. *Homemade Money* has a tremendous amount of information on advertising and marketing. If you plan on seriously making a business of sewing, check out these three sources.

Developing a List of Services and Prices

Before you embark on your business, you need to define your services, skills, and abilities. You must be objective, honest, and list *everything* you know how to do and have the equipment to achieve. List all of your skills right down to the smallest detail. Be specific. If you are good at fitting, but a specialist at fitting bras, then list this as two separate things.

After you have analyzed what you *can* do, you have to go through the list and decide what you *want* to do. If you never want to do beading, cross it off the list. Take your complete list and edit it down. Not that you should discount any of your skills, but this list will become the core of the skills you advertise. Now take this list and organize it by types of skills. For instance, list all of your hemming techniques together, all of your beading techniques together, and your special services together. This becomes your adjusted services list.

Now that your list is completed, you need to think about pricing. There are several ways of determining price. This takes practice and experience. Don't set your fees in stone but, rather, develop some general guidelines to begin with and then adjust as you gain experience working. There are two ways of determining price: by the hour and by the piece. Your advertising can state a series of hourly rates, such as:

$10 for general sewing
$15 for fitting
$20 consulting
$25 for beading

The other option is to use your hourly rate to calculate set prices for particular garment types. Remember, the prices below are labor only. So for instance:

$25 Harem Pants
$35 Straight Skirt (w/o trim)
$45 Three Panel Skirt (w/o trim)

How were these prices achieved? Let's say it takes two and a half hours to construct a pair of harem pants and your base rate is $10 per hour. That makes a pair of pants 2.5 x $10 = $25. After you have made several garments of the same type, a standardized amount of time may appear. This will allow you to develop a complete list of prices.

Personally, I use a combination of these two techniques to create a pricing sheet that accurately reflects my services. It gives my clients an opportunity to evaluate all of my skills and services and know what they are getting into financially. The worst mistake a professional seamstress can make is to undervalue or mis-represent their services. You may want to print out this list as part of your promotional materials and give a copy to each of your clients.

Selling a Product

Perhaps, rather than doing custom work, you choose to focus on pre-made garments. In this scenario, you will need capital to buy the materials and then marketing to sell the finished goods. This can be done through mail-order or in person at events. In any case, you may want to produce a catalogue of the goods you have for sale. This can be as simple as a single pricing sheet with several images to a multi-page catalogue. Many vendors offset their catalog printing costs by selling them and then deducting the cost from the first purchase.

Advertising and Marketing

When you have your own business, advertising and marketing becomes a constant and on-going prospect. If you stop advertising, your business will slow. Word of mouth is a powerful advertisement technique, but you may not want to rely on this format entirely. Each costume maker will have their own way of marketing their product, but there are some basic elements of a marketing plan that every design business needs:

Business Cards

This may seem like an obvious statement, but without a card, people will not remember your name. Business cards can be bought at a variety of different price ranges. A rock bottom card can cost as little as $10 per 1,000 at discount office supply stores. Designer cards with foil, photographs, and original art are all available. If you are just starting out, invest what you can in your cards, but don't spend a fortune. As your business grows, you can always upgrade or have several cards for different purposes.

Carry your cards with you at all times and give them to *everyone* you talk to!

Flyers

If you have a place to place flyers, make flyers. If you attend dance classes and workshops, festivals, retreats, and conventions or go to dance rummage sales, basically anywhere dancers congregate, lay out your flyers. What should you put on a flyer? List your services, list some prices, include photographs of costumes you have made, perhaps a coupon, and don't forget the contact information. If there is a dance club in your area, include your flyer in their newsletter. Many organizations offer this service for a small fee.

Magazine Advertising

There are many national, regional, and local publications that can provide a venue for advertising. You may want to do this if you are expanding your business. Ad space can be as small as a business card or up to a double-page spread. Find out what the circulation of a particular publication is in your area before investing in this type of advertising. Local or regional publications may provide a better venue than a national magazine, unless you are selling a product via mail order.

Portfolio

This is an item that can really enhance your professional image. A portfolio can be as simple as a photo album full of past designs or as complex as you like. Your portfolio is visual proof that you can do what you advertise. I have received many new clients after flashing my portfolio. They have more confidence in my work, in taking a risk in my skills, after seeing that I can complete a project and do it well. It is also a wonderful conversation piece. "Would you like to see my latest work?" "Here is my card, give me a call! I look forward to hearing from you." One item of note: make sure that your portfolio is not just an album with pictures of yourself. Even though the costume may vary, the body is the same and does not illustrate that you can work in a client/designer relationship.

Business Nuts and Bolts

The down side of running a business is taking care of the paperwork, the licenses, the permits, the taxes, and all of the other issues that have to be considered to make it a business rather than a hobby. As I stated above, there are many books that deal with these issues better than I can in this limited space. However, there are three issues that you need to consider, no matter what system you ultimately set up.

Keep Financial Records

Make sure that you keep records of what you are making, what your inventory is, and how much you have sold. I have a very simple system for keeping track of income and outflow of both materials and funds. There are software packages and numerous books that can help you set up a functional accounting system. An accountant or book keeper may be able to help develop a plan to suit your own needs. This is a complex area that every business owner will have to delve into.

Keep Client Records

Make sure to maintain a client list and reconnect with your clients through mailings or calls. In my business, each client has a folder with all of their information.

In each folder there is the same set of worksheets, including: measurement chart, illustrations of designs, contract, timsheet, supplies list, and personal information sheet. This may seem like a lot of paper, but it helps me to visualize their ideas and to help build a costume wardrobe.

Contracts

Protect yourself and your clients through the use of detailed contracts. Never release a garment until the contract has been fulfilled and payment made in full. Any changes need to be noted by both parties. If you act professionally, you will be treated professionally and a contract is the best way to ensure that both you and your client will be happy with the results. If problems arise, the contract will help you and your client resolve problems by having the goals, deadlines, and costs clearly printed out from the beginning.

Tips for Success

Below is a list of tips concerned with running a business. These are the rules that I live by and many of these issues can really impact the amount of work you can generate for yourself.

- Always look your best when meeting the public. Grooming is highly important. When I was a college student and wore jeans and tee-shirts exclusively I had trouble convincing people I knew what I was talking about.

- Wear something you have made that stands out and catches the eye. When appropriate, wear samples of your garments. A jacket, a vest, a hat, or a skirt that is unique and shows your skill as a designer will visually underscore your statements about yourself. This is especially important at events where you will meet large numbers of people. When people come up to compliment an outfit, thank them and say "This is one of my original designs. I am a costume maker, would you like to see more?"

- Carry your portfolio with you. I have two, a mini that can fit in a small bag, and my full-sized portfolio that goes with me to shows and sits on the table. I have two so that I can always have something to show.

- Laminate a business card to wear like a badge at events. This means that people walking past you will see your card and know what you do instantly. Make it easy to read from three feet, the width of a table.

- At shows, make your booth as distinctive as possible. This can mean everything from decor, such as bringing in an Oriental rug, constructing a fitting room of decorator fabric, to your choice of fabrics laid across a table to set your merchandise on.

- Display your products attractively. If items should be hung, hang them. If you have bins or baskets with items, fold them neatly. Have your display racks look neat and easy to use. Put garments on by garment type, size, or color. Make people *want* to buy your product or your services.

- If you have clients in your home, make sure your home reflects the same attention to detail that your grooming does. If your home doesn't live up to your standards, meet your clients at their homes.

- Compete in costume contests and show your work in costume shows. Get your name out into the marketplace. When you win awards, add "Award-Winning" to your flyers.

- Develop a working relationship with a well-known dancer in your area. If she is seen in one of your garments and she has a following, then chances are her students and admirers will want to hire your services.

- Working with a teacher can also be rewarding. Her students who are just getting involved in the dance will need to buy dancewear. Be there to help them make their choices, or even make the costumes for them.

- Look for opportunities to expand and diversify. If you have developed a skirt that is unique, then market the pattern, make copies and sell it, or give workshops on how to make it—or all of the above.

- Make your flyers and publicity worthy of keeping. Some dancers hold onto flyers for years simply because the pictures were inspiring. Work on making the design of your printed material eye catching, easy to read and beautiful.

- Good attitude is a must for any service oriented provider. Avoid being aloof, negative, or antagonistic. Be supportive of your clients needs and wishes and smile, *smile*, **smile** all the time.

13 Care and Handling

Once you have completed your costume, you are ready to perform. During your performance, the costume will get sweaty and dirty. Unfortunately, Middle Eastern dance costumes are often made of textiles that do not take laundering well. Many beads and most sequins will not handle more than a buffing up with damp cloth. Lamé and velvet, while dry cleanable, are often loaded up with bangles and trim that are difficult to wash. To extend the life of your costume, care for it in the manner appropriate to the materials it's constructed of. After each performance, treat your costume to some tender loving care. Develop a routine to preserve each costume piece and extend its life. Here is a quick list to get you started. Every performer has her own technique for costume preservation. Ask your favorite dancer how she keeps her costumes in mint condition.

✓ Lay your costume up to dry. Make sure that all pieces are adequately supported to avoid unnecessary strain. Mesh drying racks work well and allow for good airflow. Never put a moist or damp costume away. Mildew can eat away slowly at any natural fibers and it thrives in dark, damp fabric.

✓ If you have costume pieces you want to wash such as head scarves, body stockings, or a chemise, make sure to test wash all materials and decorations before you make them. If you have purchased these items, begin by test washing a portion by hand. Be careful in your testing. Once you have determined the best washing method, wash them as soon as you can after a performance.

✓ Make all linings removable. Put the lining on the garment last and take it out when it looks worn, smelly, stained, or damaged. The lining of the bra and belt are pressed tightly to your flesh and absorb perspiration readily. Change the linings frequently to extend the life of your garment.

✓ Inspect the surface of your garment. By spotting any food remains, tears, loose beads or coins, raveling fringe, and other loose trim, you can make the repairs or cleaning at once. If you let a stain sit, it stays. If you see a coin getting loose, you can repair it before it disappears in a whirl. Beads fall off costumes all of the time. By taking precautions ahead of time, you can prevent more of your decoration from flying away.

✓ Make a test sample composed of all materials in your costume. Hand wash this sample to see how the costume will fare through the hand washing process. If any of the beads or sequins come off, don't wash it.

✓ Many dancers use fragrant deodorant on their skin; that in turn rubs off onto their costumes. Other dancers spritz their costumes with perfume to mask unwanted body odors and keep them as fresh smelling as they are fresh looking. A light dusting of cornstarch over the lining will also do the trick. Burning candles or incense below your costume as it is airing will also freshen the garment. Another method is to use a solution of half water and half vodka in a spray bottle. Spray the inside of your costume with this solution before you dance. This is an old theatre trick that changes and cuts through the odor of perspiration.

✓ Keep perspiration off sequins and coins. Sweat can literally strip the paint off glittery surfaces. If you are placing sequins or coins in locations where they will touch the body, seal them with clear lacquer or acrylic spray paint to help protect them from harmful contact.

✓ Keep away from flames. Candles on tables, cigarettes in ashtrays, and any flaming dishes should be avoided. Not only could your costume burn or melt, so could you. Nylon and polyester will melt and stick to your skin when in close proximity to extreme heat or flame. Silk, cotton, and wool will smolder or burn. Think *safety* when you perform. Remove risks before they remove you.

✓ Don't wear the same costume over and over again. By having at least two you can rotate them, extending the life of each individual garment. This will also give you down time for each costume so you can make repairs, change linings, and revamp the decorations.

✓ Know your costume well. Nothing is sadder than to see a dancer damage her own costume during a performance. Make sure that your costume fits you well. Dance in it during practice to find out where its limitations are. Note any moves that cannot be completed safely in the costume and remove them from your routine (i.e., don't do the splits in a straight fitted skirt).

✓ Store costumes with dangling beads and bias-cut skirts by laying them flat. This may be difficult, as storage space seems to be a problem for everyone. However, gravity will pull on skirt hems and hanging beads even after the closet door is shut. Circular skirts can develop uneven hems when left to hang for long periods of time. Strands of beads can stretch too, letting the threads show, or worse yet, break.

✓ Place a desiccant such as silica gel in your storage boxes to minimize mildew and mold growth. Include a fabric bag of baking soda or cornstarch to absorb odors and moisture from the air.

Many of these tips you have heard before. Most are common sense. If you feel that you are pressed for time and cannot follow through on the care of your garment, consider the amount of money and time you have invested in it. Consider the way that a good fitting, beautiful costume can enhance your performances. Belly dancing requires an exotic as well as a professional image. Don't let your costume down and it won't let you down.

Appendix

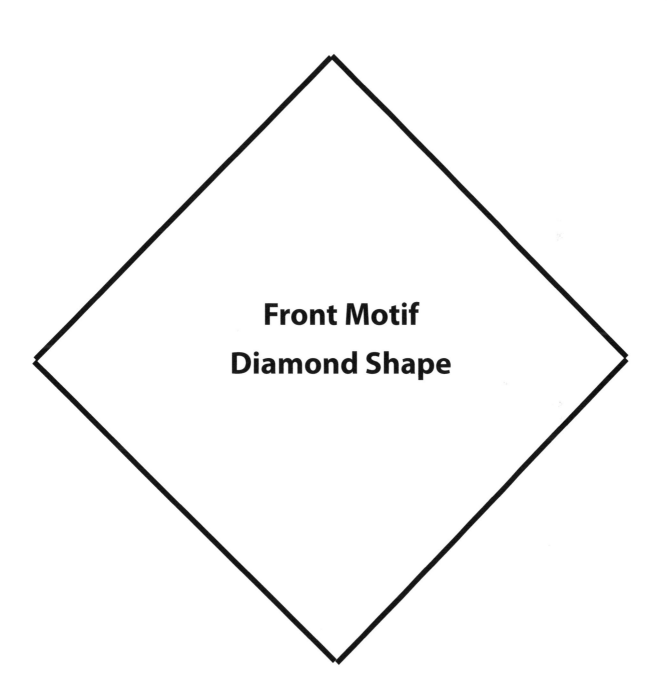

Front Motif

Diamond Shape

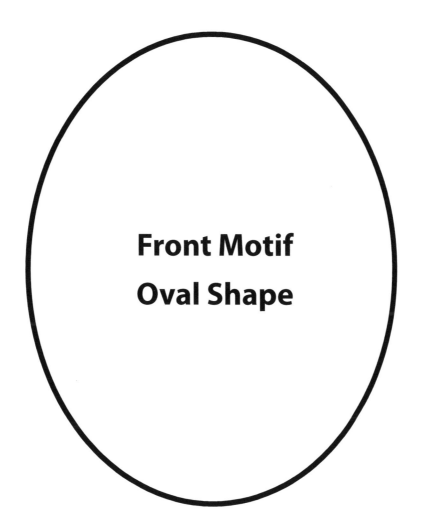

Front Motif

Oval Shape

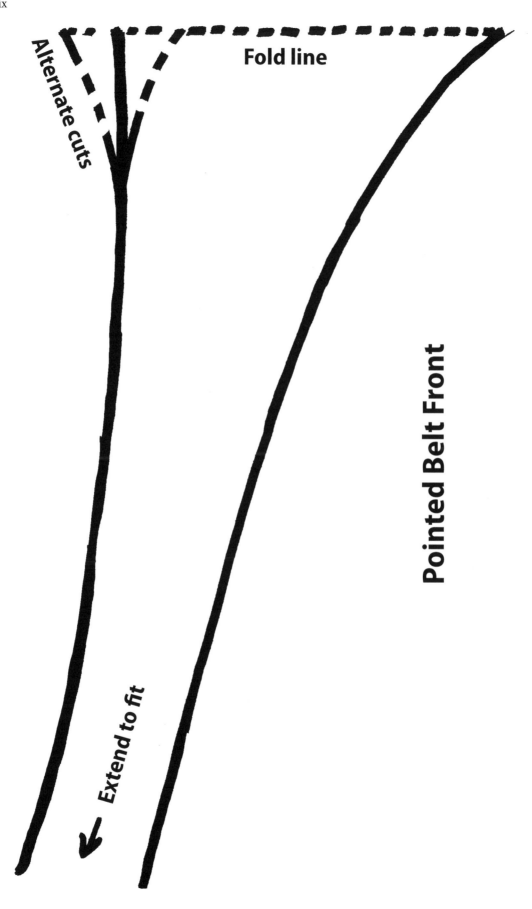

Alternate cuts

Fold line

Pointed Belt Front

Extend to fit

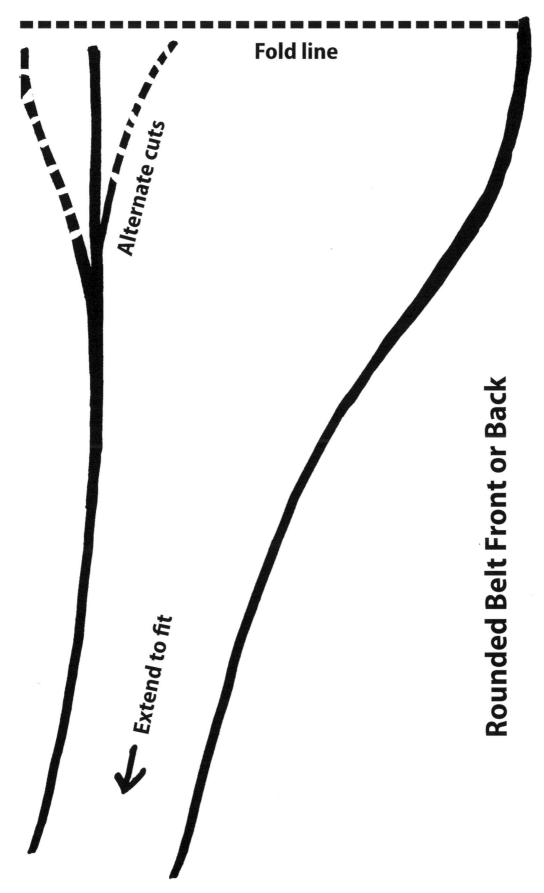

Fold line

Alternate cuts

Extend to fit

Rounded Belt Front or Back

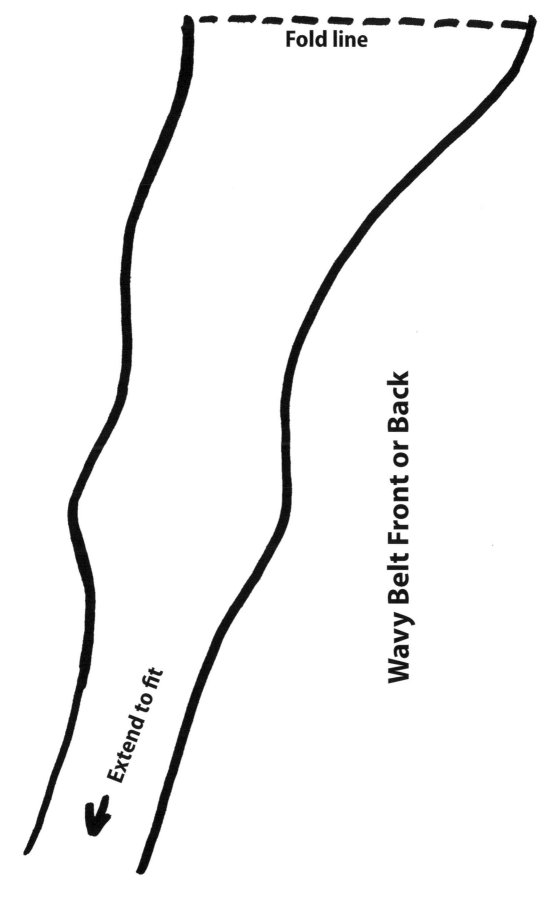

Fold line

Extend to fit

Wavy Belt Front or Back

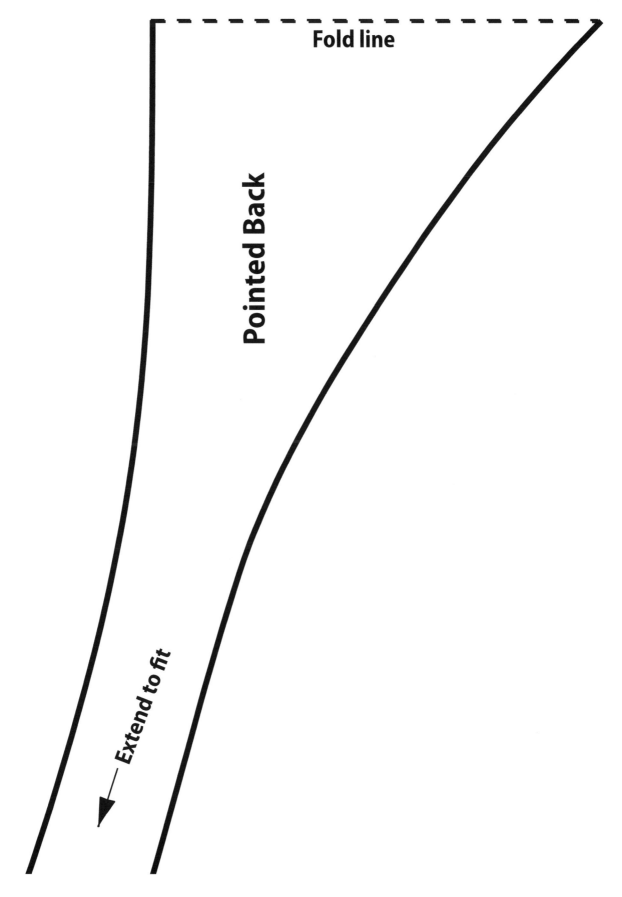

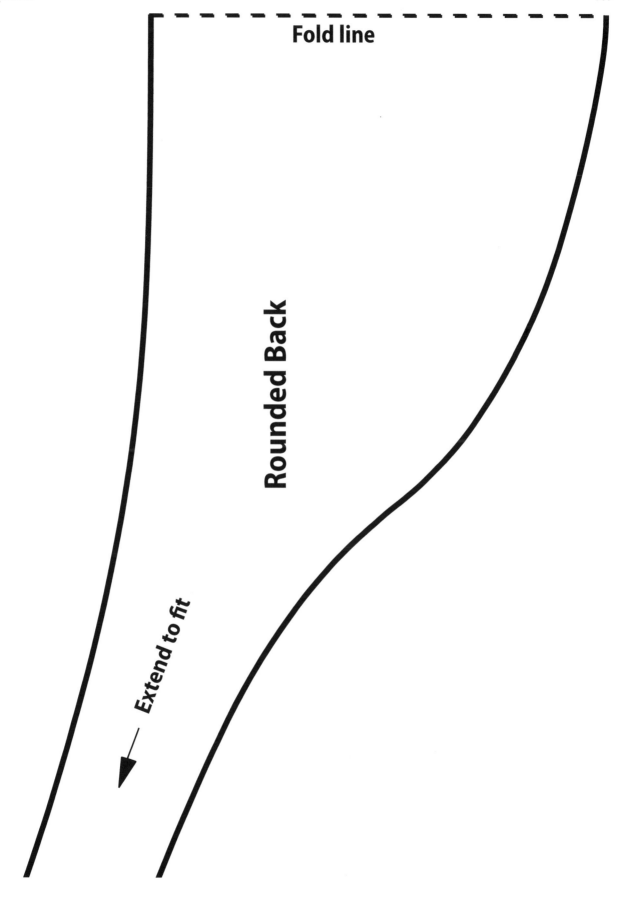

Fold line

Rounded Back

Extend to fit

Bibliography

Many people have trouble finding sources for historical research on the subject of Middle Eastern costume. Below is a portion of the bibliography that I use. Check your local public library, book store or the nearest college or university library. There are many excellent articles in magazines and journals on these subjects that are too numerous to include here.

General Costume History

Boucher, François. *20,000 Years Of Fashion.* Abrams: New York 1987.

Burnham, Dorothy K. *Cut My Cote.* Royal Ontario Museum: Onterio 1973.

Fisher, Angela. *Africa Adorned.* Collins: London 1984.

Laver, James. *Costume & Fashion: A Concise History.* Thames and Hudson: London 1985.

Maeder, Edward. *Hollywood and History.* Thames and Hudson/Los Angeles County Museum of Art: Los Angeles 1987.

Martin, Richard and Harold Koda. *Orientalism: Visions of the East in Western Dress.* Metropolitan Museum of Art: New York 1994.

Metropolitan Museum of Art. *Vanity Fair.* Metropolitan Museum of Art: New York 1977.

Museum of International Folk Art. *A Portfolio of Folk Costume, Volumes One and Two.* Museum of New Mexico Press: New Mexico 1971.

Yarwood, Dooreen. *The Encyclopedia of World Costume.* Bonanza Books: New York 1986.

Middle Eastern Costume and Textiles

Alkazi, Roshen. *Ancient Indian Costume.* Art Heritage: New Delhi 1983.

Ambrose, Kay. *Classical Dances and Costumes of India.* A. & C. Black: London 1950.

At the Edge of Asia: Five Centuries of Turkish Textiles. Santa Barbara Museum of Art: Santa Barbara, CA 1983.

Baginski, Alisa. *Textiles from Egypt, 4th–13th Centuries.* L.A. Mayer Memorial Institute for Islamic Art: Jerusalem 1980.

Baker, Patricia. *Islamic Textiles.* British Museum Press: London 1995.

Bebfoughal, T. *Les Costumes Feminins de Tunisie.* Enterprise Nationale des Arts Graphiques: Reghaia 1983.

Besancenot, Jean. *Costumes of Morocco.* Kegan Paul International: London 1990.

Bhushan. *Costumes and Textiles of India.* Taraporevala's Treasure House of Books: Bombay 1958.

Biswas, A. *Indian Costumes.* Publications Division, Ministry of Information and Broadcasting, Govt. of India: New Delhi 1985.

Bunt, Cyril G. E.. *Persian Fabrics.* Textile Book Service: Plainfield, NJ 1963.

Centre des Arts et Traditions Populaires. *Les costumes Traditionnels Feminins de Tunisie.* Maison Tunisienne de L'edition: Tunis 1970.

Clothing and Difference: Embodied Identities in Colonial and Post-Colonial Africa. Hildi Hendrickson, edt. Duke University Press: Durham 1996.

Elson, Vickie C. *Dowries form Kutch.* Museum of Cultural History, University of California: Los Angeles 1979.

From the Far West: Carpets and Textiles of Morocco. Textile Museum: Washington 1980.

King, Donald. *Imperial Ottoman Textiles.* Colnaghi: London 1980.

Mackie, Louise W. *The Splendor of Turkish Weaving: An Exhibition of Silks and Carpets of the 13th–18th Centuries.* The Textile Museum: Washington, D. C. 1973.

Markaz al-Funun wa-al-Taqalid al-Sha'biyah. *Les Costumes Traditionnels Feminins de Tunisie.* Maison Tunisienne de L'edition: Tunis 1988.

Mayer, L. A. *Mamluk Costume; a Survey.* A. Kundig: Geneve 1952.

Rajab, Jehan S. *Palestinian Costume.* Kegan Paul International: London 1989.

Reswick, Irmtraud. *Tradtional Textiles of Tunisia and Related North African Weavings.* Craft & Folk Art Museum: Los Angeles 1985.

Rogers, J. M. *The Topkapi Saray Museum, Costumes, Embroideries and Other Textiles.* Thames and Hudson: London 1986.

Ross, Heather Colyer. *The Art of Arabian Costume: A Saudi Arabian Profile.* Arabesque Commercial: Montreux, Switzerland 1981.

Scarce, Jennifer. *Embroidery and Lace of Ottoman Turkey.* Royal Scottish Museum: Edinburgh 1983.

Scarce, Jennifer. *Middle Eastern Costume from the Tribes and Cities of Iran and Turkey.* Royal Scottish Museum: Edinburgh 1981.

Scarce, Jennifer. *Women's Costume of the Near and Middle East.* Unwin Hyman: London 1987.

Spring, Christopher. *North African Textiles.* British Museum Press: London 1995.

Stillman, Yedida Kalfon. *Palestinian Costume and Jewelry.* University of New Mexico Press: Albuquerque, NM 1979.

Thomas, Thelma K. *Textiles from Medieval Egypt, A.D. 300-1300.* Carnegie Museum of Natural History: Pittsburgh, PA 1990.

Tilke, Max. *Folk Costumes from East Europe, Africa, and Asia.* A. Zwemmer: London 1978.

Uemura, Rokuro. *Persian Weaving & Dyeing.* Unsodo Publishing Co.: Kyoto 1962.

Weir, Shelagh. *Palestinian Costume.* British Museum Publications LTD: London 1989.

Woven from the Soul, Spun from the Heart: Textile Arts of Safavid and Qajar Iran, 16th–19th Centuries. The Textile Museum: Washington, D.C. 1987.

Jewelry

Andrews, Carol. *Ancient Egyptian Jewelry.* Harry N. Abrams: New York 1990.

Beck, Horace. *Classification and Nomenclature of Beads and Pendants.* George Shumway Publisher: York PA 1981.

Butor, Michel. *Ethnic Jewelry: Africa, Asia and the Pacific.* Rizzoli: New York 1994.

Coles, Janet. *The Book of Beads.* Simon and Schuster: New York 1990.

Dubin, Lois Sherr. *The History of Beads: From 30,000 B.C. to the Present.* H. N. Abrams: New York 1987.

Evens, Joan. *A History of Jewellery, 1100–1870.* Dover: New York 1970.

Hasson, Rachel. *Early Islamic Jewellery.* Institute for Islamic Art: Jerusalem 1987.

Hasson, Rachel. *Later Islamic Jewellery.* Institute for Islamic Art: Jerusalem 1987.

Higgens, Reynold. *Greek and Roman Jewellery.* Methuen and Co. LTD.: London 1980.

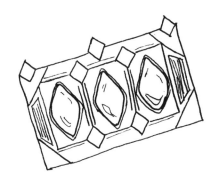

Islamic Jewelry in the Metropolitan Museum of Art. Metropolitan Museum of Art: New York 1983.

Mack, John. *Ethnic Jewelry.* Harry N. Abrams: New York 1988.

Meilach, Dona Z. *Ethnic Jewelry: Design & Inspiration for Collectors and Craftsmen.* Crown Publishers: New York 1981.

Ross, Calyer Heather. *The Art of Bedouin Jewellery, A Saudi Arabian Profile.* Arabesque: Frisbourg, Switzerland 1981.

Tait, Hugh. *Jewelry, 7,000 Years.* Abradale Press: New York 1991.

Belly Dance History and Instruction

Buonaventura, Wendy. *Serpent Of The Nile: Women and Dance in the Arab World.* Interlink Books: New York 1989.

Buonaventura, Wendy. *The Serpent and the Sphinx.* London: Virago 1983.

Carlton, Donna. *Looking for Little Egypt.* IDD Books: Bloomington, IN 1994.

Dahlena and Dona Z. Meilach. *The Art of Belly Dancing.* Bantam Books: Toronto 1975.

Gioseffi, Daniela. *Earth Dancing, Mother Nature's Oldes Rite.* Stackple Book: Harrison, PA 1980.

Mishkin, Julie Russo. *The Compleat Belly Dancer.* Garden City: New York 1973.

Nieuwkerk, Karin van. *A Trade Like Any Other: Female Singers and Dancers in Egypt.* University of Texas Press: Austin, TX 1995.

Serena and Alan Wilson. *The Serena Technique of Belly Dancing.* Pocket Books: New York 1974.

Pattern making, Construction, Surface Decoration and Sewing Business

Armstrong, Helen Joseph. *Patternmaking for Fashion Design.* Harper & Row: New York 1987.

Bensussen, Rusty. *Shortcuts to A Perfect Sewing Pattern.* Sterling: New York 1989.

Brabec, Barbara. *Homemade Money.* Betterway Publications, Inc.: White Hall, VA 1992.

Brij Bhushan, Jamila. *Indian Embroidery.* Publications Ministry, Ministry of Information and Broadcasting, Govt. of India: New Delhi 1990.

Embroidery and Lace of Ottoman Turkey. Royal Scottish Museum: Edinburgh 1983.

Grewal, Neelam. *The Needle Lore: Traditional Embroideries of Kashmir, Himachal Prdesh, Punjab, Haryana, Rajasthan.* Ajanta Publications: Delhi 1988.

Holkeboer, Katherine Strand. *Costume Construction.* Prentice Hall: Englewood Cliffs NJ 1989.

Johnstone, Pauline. *Greek Island Embroidery.* H.M.S.O.: London 1972.

Johnstone, Pauline. *Turkish Emboidery.* Victoria & Albert Museum: London 1985.

Marquand, Ed. *How to Prepare Your Portfolio.* Art Direction Book Company: New York 1981.

Morrell, Anne. *Techniques of Indian Embroidery.* B.T. Batsford: London 1994.

Paine, Sheila. *The Afghan Amulet: Travels from the Hindu Kush to Razgrad.* Michael Joseph: London 1994.

Readers Digest. *Complete Guide to Sewing.* The Reader's Digest Association, Inc.: Pleasantville, NY 1976.

Singer. *Creative Sewing Ideas.* Singer: Minnetonka, MI 1990.

Spike, Kathleen. *Sew to Success!* Palmer/Pletsch: Portland 1990.

Sykes, Barbara Wright. *The "Business" of Sewing.* Colins: Chino Hills, CA 1992.

Taylor, Carol. *Creative Bead Jewelry.* Sterling Publishing, Inc.: New York 1995.

Weir, Shelagh. *Palestinian Embroidery: A Village Arab Craft.* British Museum: London 1970.

Clip Art, Design References and Art Historical Sources

Abas, S. J. *Symmetries of Islamic Geometrical Patterns.* World Scientific: New Jersey 1995.

Akar Azade. *Treasury of Turkish Designs.* Dover Publications, Inc.: New York 1988.

Alloula, Malek. *The Colonial Harem.* University of Minnesota Press: Minneapolis 1986.

Ammoun, Denise. *Crafts of Egypt.* American University of Cairo Press: Cairo 1991.

Blackman, Winifred. *The Fellahin of Upper Egypt.* G. G. Harrap & Co. Ltd.: London 1927.

Brend, Barbara. *Islamic Art.* Harvard University Press: Cambridge, Mass. 1991.

Buourgoin, J. *Islamic Patterns.* Dover Publications, Inc.: New York 1978.

Eastern Encounters: Orientalist Painters of the Nineteenth Century. Fine Art Society, Ltd.: London 1978.

Farooqi, Anis. *Art of India and Persia.* D. K. Publishers' Distribuaters: New Delhi 1979.

Grafton, Carol Belanger. *Egyptian Designs.* Dover Publications, Inc.: New York 1993.

Hamann, Bradford R. *The Greek Design Book.* Stemmer House Publishers: Owings Mills, MA 1980.

Islam in the Balkans: Persian Art and Culture of the 18th and 19th Centuries. Royal Scottish Museum: Edinburgh 1979.

Lewis, Reina. *Gendering Orientalism: Race, Femininity and Representation.* Routledge: New York 1996.

MacKenzie, John M. *Orientalism: History, Theory and the Arts.* Manchester University Press: Manchester 1995.

Pope, Arthur Upham. *A Survey of Persian Art from Prehistoric Times to the Present.* Oxford University Press: London 1964-65.

Revault, Jactues. *Designs & Patterns from North African Carpets & Textiles.* Dover Publications Inc.: 1973.

Rice, David T. *Constantinople from Byzantium to Istanbul.* Stein and Day: New York 1965.

Rice, David T. *Islamic Art.* Praeger: New York 1965.

Thompson, James. *The East, Imagined, Experienced, Remembered: Orientalist Nineteenth Century Painting.* National Gallery of Ireland: Dublin 1988.

Thornton, Lynne. *Women as Portrayed in Orientalist Painting.* ACR Edition: Paris 1985.

Titley, Norah M. *Persian Painting: Fourteenth Century.* Marg/Arnold-Heinemann: New Delhi 1977.

Topham, John. *Traditional Crafts of Saudi Arabia.* Stacey International: London 1981.

Wilson, Eva. *Ancient Egyptian Designs for Artists and Craftspeople.* Dover Publications Inc.: New York 1987.

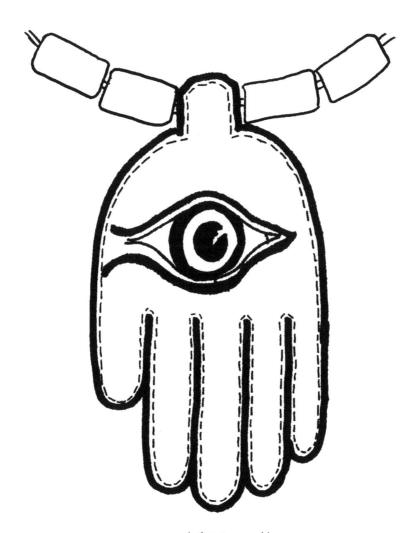

Hand of Fatima necklace.

11733116R00068